_How to Buy a Business_...

**_With_**

**_No Money,_**

**_Little Money,_**

**_the Bank's Money,_**

**_the Seller's Money_**

By K. J. Hathi

www.howtobuybusiness.com

# Disclaimer

The information contained in this book relates to a part of the author's own experience. The strategies and tips in this book are meant as a simple guide. It makes no guarantee that someone else's efforts will also produce similar results. The material can include content or information from a third party, but the author takes full charge of quoting substantial resources that may be subject to copyright issues. The author assumes no responsibility for the opinion that any of the third party or unrelated individuals have. If the content taught in the publication becomes obsolete due to technical reasons or others, the author or the publication house have no liability. All the events indicated in the book are the result of primary research, secondary research, and the personal experience of the person(s) involved in formulating the book and bringing it into the form it is in today. All the content used in this book belongs solely to the author. No part of this shall be reproduced, sold, or transmitted in any medium by the third party except after the author's approval.

# Author's Note

Yes, you read it right. How to buy businesses with No money, Little money, the Bank's money, or the Seller's money. However, most of us say, yes, that is what your book says, but it is a mere theory, all academic – it cannot happen for ME.

Well, it can happen for you – for me or anyone. I know because I did it, and I did it many times. More than 20 times in 20 years, I bought businesses with no money, little money, the bank's money, and the business seller's money.

Refer to the last pages of this book; it lists most of the businesses I have purchased. And these are not all small businesses. These are small and large businesses – some were as little as $2 million in annual sales; others were as large as $200 million in yearly sales.

Maybe you have tried to start up your own business from scratch and became quickly sour on the idea. (I did that; I found it much easier to buy an existing business). If instead you now have a desire to buy a business, this is your book. It explains the process of buying businesses – the steps you go through to do so. At times, a step may sound too simple; if it does, it probably is (life is not all sweat). At times, you will find steps challenging and frustrating. Yes, they are (life does make you work at it). All I can say is, if you have a dream and a desire to buy a business, go purchase a business! I can show you how.

Whether you buy a business with little or no money or with others' money, the process of purchasing any business, however you pay for it, remains similar. Where the money comes from is naturally important. What I am trying to say is that the money is almost always there for your purchase.

This book goes through the steps on how to find, negotiate, go through the paperwork, and buy a business. Closing the purchase of a business is the last act in buying a business. All other steps of purchasing a business that I name are essential to buying and closing a transaction.

So, go ahead, read the book – and buy a business! Good Luck!

# Table of Contents

# INTRODUCTION

Businesses continue to evolve and change. If we look at the history of the last 100 years, the companies which were prominent and established a century ago have perhaps disappeared, or new businesses emerged from the original ones, perhaps with all new products, and then they disappeared again and new companies came up.

All businesses change hands or control or form at some point in time. The change in ownership or control can happen due to the economy, the financial health of the business, due to mergers, because of the owners' desires for change (including health and succession).

For large conglomerates, one of the first significant changes came in when a company called Beatrice Foods (and other similarly large ones) got broken up and sold in pieces. The business world realized that companies like Beatrice could split up into many standalone businesses. All the subsidiaries or activities or divisions that a company owns may not have much synergy among them, yet they can be successful independent businesses. When they are split, separate companies can be worth much more than the original large company. Over the years, in creating the huge business we called Beatrice Foods, Beatrice had accumulated both small and substantial known and unknown companies – Samsonite Luggage, Tropicana, Playtex, Culligan Water, Stiffel Lamp and many more (and you see that the "Foods" part of the business wasn't all they ended up doing). When it split and those parts got sold off, these became standalone companies and either remained standalone for their entire existence or got merged with other companies.

This phenomenon was also recognized by several other large companies when they spun off parts of the business and sold them as independent businesses such as All-State Insurance by Sears, GE Appliances to Electrolux by GE, Hummer military vehicles by American General and so on.

The trend of buying, merging/acquiring and then spinning off businesses continues. Many Silicon Valley businesses nowadays like Google, Broadcom and Facebook keep acquiring companies and keep spinning them off in part or in whole. Proctor and Gamble historically bought and sold many companies and product lines. I purchased a product line called "Kirk's Castile Soap" from P&G and, for many years, operated a standalone business to distribute the product.

In the 1980s, to enhance and facilitate the financing and leveraging process, high yield corporate bonds emerged. Very soon, this was called "Junk Bonds" and became an essential financial tool to acquire businesses.

During all this time, varieties of methods to buy businesses were getting perfected. One such way was the "Leveraged Buy Out" or LBO. A leveraged buyout is a method of purchasing a company in which the buyer or buying entity leverages (uses) the assets of the target company in order to finance its purchase. I have done this, and can assure you it is not reserved for those "Big Players" only. When we say "leverage" that means to borrow funds for the purchase against the assets (collateral) of the target company – which at the time of the leveraging, the buyer does not own! The lender commits funds to the buyer on the basis of the target company's assets if closing happens. In the end, when the buyer takes possession of the assets of the target business, the lender gives committed funds for a buyout.

This form of buyout initially derived from the "receivables factoring" method. In the traditional receivables factoring method, a company sells its receivables to a financial company (called a factor). The factor itself goes out and collects payment on the receivables from the company's customers. Factoring your receivables allows your company to have ready cash quickly (rather than waiting for your customer to pay you, which might take 60, 90 days or longer). In factoring, because it transfers the title of the accounts receivable to the lender, it is about the creditworthiness of the customer whose receivables are being sold and borrowed against, and not about the credibility of the borrowing company.

During the 1980s, many LBO players became daily news to businesses such as Carl Icahn, T Boone Pickens, KKR, and many more.

The 1990s saw more of a corrective phase when businesses realized that you just *buy* it by leveraging; buying in and of itself is not necessarily a guarantee of its ongoing *success*. The massive assets of a number of companies which were funded and borrowed through "Highly leveraged transactions", started showing problems by not being capable of servicing the debts. Along came the loan delinquencies. The loan delinquencies triggered a domino effect of banks going under and became one of the biggest bank crises in US history. Through the FDIC (an independent agency created by Congress to ensure stability and public confidence in our financial system), the government had to step in to rescue delinquent banks through the Resolution Guarantee Trust.

Then came the new Millennium with its Dotcom and High-tech boom. All the rules of assets, earnings, supply and demand were ignored. Many Dotcom companies' market caps (capitalizations) skyrocketed on the perception of future value – when they didn't own a single $1 hard asset! The hard assets (real estate, inventory of physical goods, etc.) of brick-and-mortar companies such as Sears, Chicago Tribune, and United Airlines got ignored. Priceline.com and Amazon.com became bigger in market capitalization than their counterpart brick and mortar companies. Most seasoned and experienced businessmen got confused since the formulas and "rules" for values and prices seemed to have changed. Yet no one wanted to be left out of the biggest boom of the Dotcom era and it seemed that the whole country was investing in Dotcom companies. They were thinking about and reserving hundreds of names and starting companies in order not to be left out of the Dotcom gold rush. Thousands of internet businesses began in all the sectors you can think of, just to cash in. The market cap of these internet companies, due to expected future returns, went exponentially high. Millions and billions got invested in internet-based companies that were not making any money, that had no assets to speak of. This boom was ahead of its time. The Internet was new; dial-up was slow; highspeed Internet yet to come.

The concept was valid if you look at the current trend of US-founded Amazon or China's Alibaba; at that time of 25 years ago though, it was ahead of its time – and on shaky ground. As time went by, we were seeing our largest retail businesses with very little brick and mortar.

Many internet start-up businesses at that time started facing difficulties. Then came the meltdown of Dotcom in 2000, and that brought us back to reality. Dotcom euphoria and many Internet companies wiped out billions of dollars of value during early 2000. Out of ten Internet businesses, one survived while the other nine either merged or folded. In the past as well, changing technology saw high-tech companies experience similar difficulties by being ahead of their time. Microsoft's Bill Gates and Apple's Steve Job had fueled hundreds of computer companies in the 70s; a few survived but many failed.

When you look back now from the year 2020, computer companies, software businesses, the Internet boom, and Dotcom boom were not fake or imaginary. They were just ahead of their time. Once things shook out, with many businesses folded and relaunched, they were organized and became bigger than ever. Amazon, Google, Facebook, and so on became the largest companies, beyond even their counterpart brick and mortar businesses. Today, there are brokers who sell website-only businesses for up to many, many millions of dollars. You can purchase a business like that, surely. By now the basic rules have returned and are obeyed: Business is for profit, business is supply and demand, business is both hard and soft assets, business is the name, the brand and the products, business is service and fulfillment.

All along those years, Internet technology was improving, and in the background, Internet-related businesses and high-tech were picking up momentum. Internet and high-tech started penetrating in every phase of brick-and-mortar, service and professional, manufacturing and all types of company operations, making businesses ever more efficient and profitable. It took hold in finance through online trading, online travel (reservations for air, hotel and car) and the online sale of valuable items like vehicles and homes. There is tech for traffic safety, and for managing your home in your absence. We are at the point now that we cannot be without Internet connectivity and service provided by any company over the internet. An example of that is my children and theirs – they cannot choose a restaurant to dine at without consulting the online reviews for it first!

So whichever internet businesses survived or launched, a number of them became giants – Amazon, Microsoft, Apple, Google, Facebook, etc. As I said earlier, as time goes by, this will also change given time, and will continue to improve over what we experience today.

However, the fundamentals of buying a business are almost unchanged – what is important is the *product, process, services, demand and supply, and making a profit.* Business ownership and business buying have remained similar throughout all these decades of technological changes. The purchase price of business is affected by the product, profit, technology and other factors, but the components of any business-buying process stay relatively stable.

In this book, I will go over the business buying process, as a guideline for you in your own selection and purchase of a company. Because hopefully, you are in the market to acquire a business!

# Chapter 1: Where and How to Find a Business for Sale

In theory, most businesses are for sale. The questions are: When is it for sale? How much to pay for it? How to find such businesses?

To locate businesses for sale is the first step in the process of buying a business. In this chapter, I will discuss finding and buying businesses of all sizes and revenue levels. I will consider buying from individual owners, from companies or corporations, including large conglomerates and out-of-bankruptcy opportunities.

Most of the necessary steps of purchasing businesses remain the same whoever the owner and whatever their circumstances; however, the buyer needs to adjust and fine-tune the process to fit the type of business and its sellers.

Small Businesses

Individuals or families generally own small businesses as a sole proprietorship, as an LLC or other incorporated form.

Many times, the owner does not have a family to whom to pass his or her business, or the children are not interested (no succession plan). Sometimes, the owner is just burnt out, worked too hard for the company, and now wants to quit. Retirement and moving elsewhere can be other significant reasons. It is also common that many companies are available after they had a good year or a few good years and the owner believes he can get the maximum selling price. Sometimes, a business is available for sale because its revenue is decreasing or the owner knows/senses that it will decrease more. If anyone knows the future problems of that business, the owner knows them best! Say that he knows his product line is diminishing in customers' eyes (decreasing demand) or import competition is coming (increasing pressure on price or quality), the owner then may want to sell.

Some businesses, interestingly, may not be actually for sale (yet you may still be able to buy them) when they are "put on the market". The owner may only be testing the market for interest in his business and for sale price amount.

Some businesses may be for sale, but cost you too much. Or, after spending a considerable amount of research, energy, time and money, you may still not be able to buy it. This can happen when "the business is the owner's life", and he gets cold feet at the last moment when it is time to close the sale and sign the documents. He starts thinking, "What will I do tomorrow?" The owner backs out. This is common with a founder-owner who has spent all his or her life in establishing the business.

In October 1983, I bought a manufacturing business, Aetna Pipe

Products of Illinois, in Chicago, from the owner's estate.

After I bought it, I met several people who said that they'd also wanted to buy that business. A number of them had gone very far in negotiating their purchase. However, at the last minute, the seller backed out or found a reason for not selling it. After talking to those failed buyers, I realized that I was able to successfully buy the business only because the owner had passed away and his widow did not or could not operate that type of manufacturing company.

I purchased Aetna Pipe with bank financing. I invested ten percent, which was $85,000 of my own money, and the bank lent me the remaining 90% on the total purchase price of $850,000. The business had two plants with real estate owned (REO), lots of machinery and equipment, good inventory, and accounts receivable. Those were strong assets for the bank to use as collateral on my loan! The previous owner did not have any loans but used the same bank that financed me. The bank wanted to retain that account, so when they knew I was looking at it, they funded me very generously. After my buyout, the bank maintained our accounts. This buyout was "a typical bank-financed transaction with little money."

<u>Medium and Large Businesses:</u>

Public companies and large companies have different reasons for coming onto the market for sale. Once a company is big, they may not have many resources or do not want to deal with small businesses they have within their corporate or holding structure, so they sell the small businesses (subsidiaries or divisions of the larger corporation, most of the time) or individual product lines. Sometimes, they sell to raise cash to operate or increase their core business (or to cover other irritating debts they have). When two companies merge, or one business acquires another one, they see that redundancy is created in the businesses. By that we mean two payroll departments or two marketing departments and so on (and carrying two when you need only one is expensive). Those businesses get sold or discontinued. Sometimes, to avoid monopoly, when a company buys another one in a similar industry, the Federal Trade Commission (FTC) may not allow buying unless the buyer sells part of the acquired industry off to avoid a monopoly situation.

Medium and large companies may be sold variously through investment bankers, accountants, lawyers, commercial/retail bankers, business brokers, vendors, customers or by word of mouth. Note that publicly traded companies usually hire investment bankers to sell their companies.

This said, some large companies have an internal department whose only job is to buy and sell businesses. I purchased a soap company from a large conglomerate, Proctor and Gamble, which was sold to me by their in-house department. In the late 80s, Bethlehem Steel had its in-house group market their businesses. They sold two companies to me. They also hired a large New York-based investment banker to sell another company which I bought.

In my experience, the negotiating process with investment bankers is complicated and unpredictable, depending on the firm representing the seller. By profession and training, investment bankers take longer with some decision-making processes. Inside corporate managers are usually more straightforward, more comfortable and faster to run through the process. If they determine that you are a genuine and serious buyer, the transaction becomes easier.

Let us discuss various professionals who can help you to identify businesses for sale.

<u>Accountants:</u>

The business accountant/CPA or accounting firm of the company for sale probably knows more about the business than everyone except for the seller. If the seller does decide to sell, usually the accountant knows. Whether the sale is due to losses in the business, lack of a successor, owner health or retirement, declining sales or any other reason, accountants are generally aware of the reason for it. Accountants are usually not brokers. In fact, by nature, accountants are more conservative than brokers. Due to their professional training, their knowledge of the business is typically accurate.

When looking for available companies to purchase, it is a good idea to talk to some accountants whose practice is geared more to a business clientele than to individual clientele.

If an accountant or accounting firm helps in selling a business, their interest is to retain the account of business with a new owner, so keep that fact in mind.

<u>Bankers:</u>

If a bank finances the business, bankers will be well-tuned with that business. If the company has debt, the banker usually knows the performance of the business. If the business is not doing well, the banker, most of the time, remembers. The reason a banker comes to know is either because the company missed a debt payment or has experienced some delays making periodic loan payments. Usually, the banker advises the owners what to do with the business if the business is facing difficulty. The business bank usually has a large number of companies in its portfolio, which they finance. They may know at any given time the number of businesses that might be available for sale. One must approach the banker to ask for companies available for purchase. Usually, unless they know you, they will not volunteer to discuss a business for sale. They also typically have a feeling if any business is soon coming available for purchase. Due to confidentiality issues, they do not disclose financial details of any company to you. However, if you convince the banker that you are a genuine prospect as a buyer, and you have resources and a good reputation, they will introduce you to the seller. If you referred by a bank, it is an excellent start for any buyer (and for the seller, for that matter), as it somewhat establishes a buyer's creditworthiness or ability to buy a business. If you approach a banker and they say they do not know any business for sale, just continue asking him or her from time to time. Their other branches may know of some for sale. They may have other banking contacts who may also see companies for sale. They may bring up the success or failure story of a company, which can give you a hint to how to approach them. Sometimes they may provide you leads but will not introduce you. Bankers are an excellent source, but it a difficult source, as, after all, their main business is not buying and selling businesses. Banks intend to retain the account if the seller is their client or to gain an account if the seller is not their client.

Brokers:

Business brokers are an excellent source to learn which businesses are available; unlike bankers, this is in fact their core business activity. Business brokers are less regulated by states, unlike real estate brokers, who are also a reasonable sources of finding companies for sale.

Business brokers maintain lists of potential businesses for sale. Once he finds the right buyer, he often asks the buyer to sign a confidentiality agreement and a fee agreement. Some business brokers charge a fee to sellers, while some charge one to buyers. I have come across cases where business brokers charge commissions to both sides after disclosing the dual relationship to buyer and seller. Usually, being professionals, brokers have better packages of businesses for sale than accountants, bankers, and lawyers – after all, this is their bread-and-butter activity. Some real estate brokers, when they are selling the building which houses an operating company, may offer a business for sale on behalf of the owner/seller.

Due to the internet, there are now many online brokers, websites and investment listings of all types of businesses. Businesses listed by brokers are priced to market level and not necessarily a "bargain" for a buyer. It has another layer of cost on top of the purchase price, which is the broker's compensation. At the same time, if the broker has been sitting on that business for sale for an extended period, you may get it for much less than the listed price (much like a home on the market for months will reduce its sale price to attract buyers). If you are registered with a broker as a buyer, the broker might bring it to your attention if the seller becomes desperate to sell.

Newspapers and Media:

Many publications have sections for "Business For Sale" like Wall Street, Investment Daily, USA Today, local papers, etc. Many weekly and monthly business newspapers also have a part where they advertise a business for sale such as Chicago Tribune, Crain's Chicago Business.

Because of online growth, websites, and search engines, there are fewer print newspapers that have those sections today. But besides their "businesses for sale" classified ads, daily news articles are rich sources of companies for sale. You may read some articles and news reports which say

15

a large corporation is selling some of its businesses. Read the article to find out if the larger business plans to sell (another term for this is "divest themselves of") a whole business subsidiary or only one or more of its activities or product lines. You have got to dig in and study the articles to learn what is happening and if you might be interested. You can directly approach the industry; you do not need an intermediary. The Chief Financial Officer or CFO of the company is usually in charge of selling or buying details.

Lawyers:

Most businesses are a client of lawyer/law firms for one reason or another during their existence.

Lawyers may find out a business is for sale due to death, judgment, a bank calling in a loan, bankruptcy filing, or owner estate planning.

If the owner is selling a business, most owners usually do not tell lawyers initially; however, if a buyer comes, the owner will seek a lawyer's advice about documentation. They must notify lawyers if it becomes public knowledge, or if the business is facing difficulties.

Bankruptcy lawyers are mostly selling or restructuring businesses. Many times, if a business files bankruptcy under Chapter 11 and cannot restructure, it may get liquidated under Federal Bankruptcy Code Section 363. In this case, the court sells the business to a highest bidder with the best offer. I have bought several companies this way. If you buy under a Section 363 bankruptcy sale, it is usually all cash. The advantage, though, is that the purchase price will be low, deeply discounted, pennies on the dollar.

<u>Investment Bankers:</u>

Investment bankers are brokers who offer other services besides buying and selling businesses. They may provide financing services such as raising debt, pension plans, consolidations of finance-related areas and they might advise on the tax ramifications of buying or selling businesses.

When I was buying a company from Bethlehem Steel Corporation and speaking to one of the bankers, I called him a "broker", and he got all bent out of shape. He told me, "We are not brokers, we are investment bankers."

To me, however, they were performing a broker's role. They were not financing the company or finding financing for me. They had prepared the company's offering memorandum and package and were representing the seller to sell the company.

Investment bankers are an excellent source of companies that are for sale. Being large, they have many businesses for sale all the time. They tend to be larger businesses; however, you find some small businesses on offer. The bankers who represent large clients will also sell small companies for their large clients as a "one-stop shopping" service to them.

If you are a new buyer, it is usually hard to get a package from these large houses unless you can make them comfortable that you have resources yourself (or have lined them up with others) to complete the transaction. They typically send you a teaser about the business for sale, with minimal information and without the name of the company. Once you review and tell them that you like it, they will ask you to send them your financial statement or bank references to prove that you can complete a transaction of that size. After that, they will send you a confidentiality agreement followed by a package or offering memorandum.

Investment bankers are an excellent source of larger companies for sale. Many big names such as the old Bear Sterns, Goldman Sachs, Morgan Stanley are large investment bankers. There are smaller, somewhat more regional, investment bankers as well and you can find them in most regions, though some of these firms have disappeared or merged.

Business owners of the Baby Boomer generation – and there are lots of them coming up in this millennium – are looking to retire, "take the money and go fishing", so businesses continuously come onto the market for sale.

Approaching Brokers or Sellers:

The right approach with a broker or a seller is essential. Once you know the business is for sale, if there is a middleman (a broker or investment banker), you should approach them properly. Then they qualify you to receive a confidentiality agreement and eventually a package (by "package" I mean a collection of informational documents about the business for sale, that the seller has prepared for prospective buyers). The broker and the seller then need to be satisfied that you have ready funds or a bank's backing and that you can close the deal.

How do you do that? If you have lots of money and proven track records of buying many companies, you just give your banker's name and the names of the businesses you bought in the past. However, that is usually not the case. Often, you do not have the total purchase price in liquid cash. Even in the case you do, you do not want to put all the money up as equity – keep some in your pocket! So, you will have – or want to spend out of your pocket – a limited amount of money.

Let us say that a business is available for sale for $20,000,000. You have anywhere between $100,000 to $5,000,000. Or even worse, you have only $50,000. In any of the above cases, you need a banker or a reputable finance company. A banker who finances that type of company can give the seller or broker a comfort level about you with one phone call.

I have bought businesses where my equity has been anywhere from 1% to 100% of the purchase price. Once you supply your equity information and the bank references, usually, a broker will work with you.

By going through this book's next chapters, you will learn how banks generally finance that business. Once you have that number, add your equity number and come up with a purchase price. If you still have a shortfall, you may use a mezzanine lender (Mezzanine debt is also called subordinated debt, and is typically provided by a third party "Mezzanine" lender, not the bank or a private equity firm) or a less complicated seller note. You usually do not talk of seller note or mezzanine lending until the transaction progresses further.

# Chapter 2: Buying versus Starting a Business

I started my career as a salaried engineer, and worked from 1973 to 1983 for Union Carbide Corporation setting up various manufacturing plants across US and world. But, being an entrepreneur by nature, I tried to start several companies during my employment with Union Carbide. Also, being an electrical engineer by education, I enjoyed playing around with gadgets. I came up with a variety of devices, and one of them in the 1970s was an automotive aftermarket device which turned on car headlights when it was dark and off when it was bright outside. At that time, Cadillac offered this device in new cars only. We came up with how to do it ourselves for any vehicle; our unit was compact and low cost. A friend and I made some sample units and received favorable feedback from the initial market research. The prototypes worked, and we produced about a thousand units in our garage against an order. The product was well designed and technically worked well.

Engineers and inventors are breeds by themselves, and my friend and I, both being engineers, were not any different. The way we thought was that the product is right, it's working, and now all the major work is done. The product was complicated and we had to prepare a big chart of the various models of cars, hundreds of them. It included an instruction sheet (in length) to explain how to install the device under the dashboard. We thought that now it was just a matter of racking up money.

Well, it was surprising. First, the skill of an average consumer who installs an aftermarket light device of this nature is just not there. To go under the dashboard, to pull the light switch out, splice 6 to 10 wires (color-coded to make things easier) was just impossible. Whoever would try to hook it up very rarely succeeded. We had some angry customers, calling us and complaining that when it gets dark, his horn comes on. We had units returned, and very fast we ran out of the small savings which we had invested. Sadly, our business folded.

After that, I started several similar other small businesses which likewise failed. Then I bought my first fully operational business! What a difference! My personal experience says that buying an on-going business is far better than starting a business from nothing.

When you purchase an on-going business, the complete infrastructure comes with it. It comes with a name, experienced people, plant, equipment, machine tools, dies, design, maintenance schedule, work practices, accounting practices, schedules, vendors, customers, stationery, product literature brochures, vehicles, purchasing, and the list goes on and on.

An on-going business has been there, through ups and downs. It took years to get established and has weathered many storms. If it's your own start-up business, it takes many more years of blood, sweat and tears to get organized and to really profit.

Statistically, four out of five startup companies fail in the first two years or so! The mental and financial impact of failure after working so hard is so great that you usually would not start again. Not only won't you want to start the next new business, you will be afraid of buying an existing one as well. Don't be. It is much easier to buy an existing business!

Of course, in a startup, there are many success stories like Bill Gates, Steve Jobs, and many others. However, remember that ninety percent of startup businesses fail, and you never hear about them. The road of startup businesses is full of landmines, with dead companies buried everywhere.

When you buy an ongoing business, you are not starting anything from scratch; only the owner has changed, not the company. The company is intact; someone else has put in his or her blood, sweat, and tears. Someone else has worked hard, and you are benefiting. The company, over the years, has gone through cyclical highs and lows and survived. In my view, it is far easier to operate an on-going business than to start one up!

I guess when the new entrepreneur does not have any or much capital to invest and wants to go into business, the first thing he thinks of is to start a business "on a shoe-string". Instead I show you how to buy a business – also with little of your own money.

I fell by chance into buying my first business, Aetna Pipe Products of Illinois. I did not plan to purchase. A contact of mine introduced me to his friend; he wanted an equipment appraisal of a business that he was planning to buy. My contact knew my job at Union Carbide. It was primarily setting up equipment and plants. He also knew that I had sent a fully operating bakery plant to Kenya in East Africa, moved a disposable diaper plant in Germany and a number of plants in the USA for the company I worked for. So, he asked me if I could help him to understand the equipment. It is also likely he did not want to pay for an equipment appraisal, or he did not know anyone – but I was game! I went to see the machinery in the plant and gave him accurate advice that this was old equipment but good enough for the job it was doing. They were made of heavy steel so it would outlast both of us as long as he kept them running and in good repair.

He took my advice, and he entered negotiations with the seller. Well, he started negotiating with the seller, who had started the business from scratch. The seller was saying that he wanted to sell, but he in fact did not want to. Every time, the seller had different reasons not to sell (at least that is what I heard later on). While negotiation of this transaction was going on, the seller passed away.

Suddenly, now the buyer had to negotiate with the seller's widow. The buyer now thought that he would have his way. He became greedy, started reducing the purchase price, assuming he was the only game in town, and I believe he was. The buyer had done all the work and negotiated an asset-based loan through Main Bank. As time went by, he started negotiating harder and harder with the widow. After a couple of times doing price reductions, the seller's widow got tired. She threw the buyer out and told him that she did not want to sell the company to him at any price.

Later on, she approached me through the bank and I acquired the business, and the same lender financed me with 10% down.

That is where I realized the beauty of purchasing an operating business versus investing in a startup. The company had two small plants and was in the pipe cutting and threading business. It was a low-tech small business with an understandable product line. In the first few days, I got familiar with the company. The company had all the ingredients of a well-run business: It had a product line, customers, vendors, machinery and equipment, plants, an accounting department, and 25-plus well-experienced employees.

After a few days, I realized that the business did not need me. If it were a start-up, to reach that size would have taken me many years, not a few months. My conclusion? My experience was better at purchasing an established business! This does not mean that I do not respect start-ups and the significant potential of startups. All the Google, Facebook, Amazon, Microsoft, Apples were start-ups and made significant money and have impacted the markets in many ways. My first reservation is about the low percentage of success with startups versus the great potential for continuing success with an on-going business.

# Chapter 3: Types of Businesses

There are all types of businesses. This is manufacturing, service, distribution, retail, professional, etc. However, all companies have the same common goal: Make Profit.

The IRS says that the business's expenses are tax-deductible only if the business makes a profit. After a certain number of years, if it does not make a profit, it is considered a hobby and not a company.

Let's be realistic; if you are going to own a business, you will own it because it is profitable – or to make it so. The company can be made cost-effective and profit-producing in many ways, such as merging, growing, cutting expenses, getting better product lines, different sales approaches, repositioning to enter new markets and so on. "If your ship has a hole, either you plug it or get out of the ship, because it is going to sink," someone once said. If you continue losing money, your business will fail.

So now, when you are buying a business, make sure that it is profitable or can be made profitable. As we said before, if you cannot make it so, it will die. Are you always sure that it would become profitable? Not necessarily.

There will always be risk, and one should take the risk. However, if you conclude that it cannot be made profitable (or that you just don't know how to achieve that), don't do it; do not buy it.

At the same time, if you want 100% assurance that you will buy only a profitable business, then your chances of buying a business at all are minimal to none. By nature, a company cannot guarantee being productive; maybe a very few can say so, and it may cost you a fortune to buy them.

If we sincerely believe in business and its profitability as its guiding buying/owning criteria, the type of business and location really takes a backseat. Any legitimate company may be acceptable. Sometimes a business may be legitimate and profitable; however, your ethics and belief may also decide what not to buy. In my case, being vegetarian, I would not buy or get involved with the meat industry. You may have different convictions and beliefs.

Most of the time, it is not the *type* of business that becomes profitable or loss-making. With two companies of the same type, one may be making a profit, and the other may be losing money. The profit or loss of business may depend on its market positioning and market share, revenue administration, management and selling skill, operational effectiveness, expense/cost controls, products/services quality or perceived value, etc. You have to look at it all!

<u>Manufacturing</u>:

Manufacturing businesses make/produce physical products. It can be any kind of product. Nowadays, people think the manufacturing industry is in decline. Manufacturing is not dead! Lately, in the modern era of the Internet, with e-products and virtual businesses, we forget about actual products and think that e-products are the products. Millions and millions of hard products are made daily around the world, and manufacturing businesses make them. Some products are used every day, some are consumed every day, some go into making other products, and so on.

When you are looking to buy a business, there are primarily three types of manufacturing businesses. One which manufactures products with brand names; a second without any brand name, which puts no name or someone else's name on the item; a third which has a brand name and also makes unbranded products; in other words it is a combination of the first and second kind.

<u>Branded Manufacturing Company</u>: These companies usually have strong name recognition of their products in the marketplace and with consumers. Products such as Glad Bags, Tide Detergent, Dial Soap, Cadillac, Xerox, Kleenex, Kellogg's, etc. These companies may or may not have production facilities. They must control their production and quality to protect the brand's reputation. Furthermore, some of them, when they cannot meet demand, get partial products made outside. Specifications and the quality of the product are outsourced; some of these "manufacturers" do

not have any manufacturing facilities. Quality is controlled through their own internal standards.

For any business, product manufacturing, whether inhouse or contracted out, changes as demand and supply changes. For example, let us say a product line has the right profit margin and a large production plant. There may not be enough volume to support the overhead of the plant for a limited amount of production volume (in times of low product demand). So the company, to enhance profitability, may sell or shut down the plant and transfer the production to a third party called a Co-Packer or Toll manufacturer. This way, they retain profitability. Usually, the outside world still has a perception of the company as a manufacturer; however, they simply own the brand.

In 1995, I purchased Kirk's Castile Soap brand from Proctor & Gamble. Kirk's Castile had been a brand name since 1839. The company had high gross margins and was profitable. However, it was a declining market and a small brand in that market; I sold it to another brand name competing company the same year. When I acquired Kirk's, Kirk Soap was made in the P&G plant in the Philippines. We did not purchase the plant; however, we acquired Kirk's Castile Brand only and started buying the product from the contract manufacturer (Hewitt in Dayton, Ohio; later from Valley Products in Memphis, TN; then from Guatemala).

All these companies are primarily contract packagers, not manufacturers. However, we were perceived by the consumer as a manufacturing company. Many large manufacturers do not have plants; they outsource their products to domestic or international manufacturers.

Contract Packager or Non-Branded Manufacturer:

These companies are usually product manufacturers of a commodity type of item (a standardized product that is the same from one producer to another). Often, they do not have any brand, or only a weak brand called white-label or house label. These companies typically make generic (commodity) products such as nuts and bolts, textiles, soap, paper goods, and many other commonly used products. These products are supplied directly to the market or to branded companies which place the brand name on the products that rise to the company's standards of quality.

These companies' contract manufacturers have high fixed costs due to their brick-and-mortar manufacturing plants and equipment. Sometimes, the customers, if a branded company, may provide partial or complete raw material to the contract packager. At that time, the contract packagers have less or no inventory exposure. In this case, the contract packager makes its money charging plant overhead and labor. Sometimes retailers such as Wal-Mart, Target, Walgreens or Costco may come to contract packagers and ask them to supply complete products under their names such as Equate (a Wal-Mart controlled brand), or under the Walgreens name. In this case, sometimes a contract packager purchases raw materials, makes the product, stores finished products and releases product upon a customer request or a standard distribution/delivery agreement. Many times, the customers may cancel the orders or go bankrupt, and the contract packager may not be able to sell the products. The contract packager also has a low overall gross margin and volatile business volume fluctuation as they do not control brand names. As a standard business practice, the branded products company does the marketing and advertising, while the contract manufacturer provides the finished, packaged and labeled product only.

When you are acquiring a manufacturing company, the following are essential aspects of business for buying and financing purposes.

- A manufacturing business tends to have more physical assets. It usually has a real estate, land, and buildings (owned or leased), machinery, equipment, tools, dies, fixtures, accounts receivable, inventory, goodwill, trademarks, trade name, patents, trade secrets, trade expertise, and other hard and soft assets.

- If it is a profitable business, a manufacturing business is generally more comfortable to finance because it has more hard assets. Banks may fund 70% of the appraised value of land and building. You may let the seller hold the financing for the real estate. If the seller holds funding, it is usually a more comfortable and faster transaction. Otherwise, the lender will require an EPA report and MIA (Member Appraisal Institute) appraisal of the lenders' choice, which you will pay.

- You will also be able to finance accounts receivable for about 75 to 85% of outstanding good receivables that are under 90 days of aging. Over 90 days, outstanding accounts are considered "aged" or risky to collect by banking standards.

- You may be able to borrow around 30% to 60% against good turning inventory depending on your products and the lender's ability to liquidate.

- The lender will finance the finished product or raw materials, which can be easily liquidated by the lender. Work in progress and packaging material is generally not funded by the lender due to the inability to sell it.

Many of the businesses I purchased were financed based on the above method of borrowing. When you go through the due diligence process on the business you are buying, you get a rough idea of how much you may be able to borrow. Once you know what you can get in loan monies, add the cash equity that you are willing to put in, and that is the purchase price. Then start negotiating with the seller. If you still have a shortfall of the purchase price, you can ask the seller to take a percentage of the selling price as a note. This note is usually a subordinated note to bank borrowing. Banks prefer it when the seller takes a note, as it is considered pseudo equity.

Manufacturing businesses tend to have more employees in their production lines. Expertise in manufacturing is the heart of the company. If talented people are not there or leave upon your buying of the business, building the product becomes difficult. To make a product, the equipment must be there; the plant should be there; the skilled and unskilled employees should be there. Once all those work in harmony, the product becomes valuable.

My manager at Aetna Pipe once said to me, "Manufacturing is like a mechanical clock. Every gear must link with each other precisely all day every day. If it does not, the output time of the clock is useless." In the same way, all manufacturing, people, process, and the equipment must work together. Productivity must be there to make a competitive product.

Pricing and quality and value must be there so that a customer buys your product and not a competing one. The shipping must be on time to have the product on the shelf when a customer needs it. When you produce the product, your inventory of the components, raw material, work in process, and finished products must be right. Otherwise, you may have a shortfall or excess products. The billing department must check the credentials of the customer, otherwise the company may never get paid. Accounting must keep track of precise cost and profitability, otherwise you may never know if you are making money or losing it, and you may not have funds to operate the business. There are many more elements in the manufacturing business and all of them must work just like a mechanical clock to manage a manufacturing company. Otherwise, the output is worthless.

The US manufacturing base has deteriorated drastically due to fierce international competition, true. High labor costs and heavy regulatory requirements (such as EPA, OSHA, etc.), product liabilities and labor laws have been major factors for the deterioration of US manufacturing. The change of product cycles, either being phased out or wholly discontinued, makes it harder for manufacturers worldwide. Don't be fooled: There are still buying opportunities.

I acquired Aetna Pipe Products in 1983. The company was in Chicago and had two plants. I owned 100% of the company. The company consisted of two plants with an annual revenue of $2 million. The company was operated profitably for 10+ years and sold to competition in 1996.

Chicago at that time had around ten or so large lamp-and-lighting product manufacturers. There were some large and well-known companies such as Stiffel Lamp, Bradley Lamp, and others. By the late 1980s, Taiwan started selling lighting parts in the US at a much lower cost. So, to cut costs, certain manufacturers around the nation started buying the components and subassembly directly (straight from Taiwan and Korea) or through distributors. With Aetna being component manufacturers of tubing and pipes which are used in lamps, we felt price pressure. Our prices of steel fabrication of tubing and pipe due to union wages were high. On top of it, finishing companies such as brass, chrome, and zinc plating companies got hit with costly and stringent requirements of EPA compliance. This regulatory requirement put several companies out of business and the ones who survived raised prices. The regulatory requirements in the US again gave the Taiwanese an edge for competing.

One time, I went to Taiwan to source some high labor plated parts for our company; they sold me finished parts cheaper than I could buy raw steel! As time went by, it became worse. China and Taiwan started selling complete products. There was no more need for part manufacturers. We sold our small Aetna Pipe business to the competition at a substantially discounted price.

These manufacturers' stories run through all sectors for almost all products. Will they come back? Maybe, but more automated. And if there are trade restrictions against foreign low labor imports.

Distribution Business:

Usually, the distribution business's primary assets are warehouses, equipment, inventory, and accounts receivable. To buy and finance distribution businesses, one should look into the following areas.

If the business owns the building (real estate), there will probably be financing available against the building. Local lenders and regional banks usually do building financing. In the regular profitable distribution business, 70% of the funding against the appraised value of the real estate should be standard. Against good inventory and accounts receivable, financing is also available. Accounts receivable in most business financing can be around 75-85% with clean accounts receivable. The inventory in distribution usually is comprised of only finished product, and lenders are more comfortable in lending against it. Provided it is not slow-moving and outdated, the lender should finance 45-65%. The company should own this inventory.

Modern distribution businesses have increased in number. The distribution supply chain has become a significant factor in the growth of big-box retailers such as Walmart, Target, and others. The critical factor in this business is an efficient distribution system and sourcing. It tends not to be labor intensive. The commodity type of distribution sees volatile price fluctuations and many hidden characteristics which can slip out of your control.

When I acquired a distribution business named Bethlehem Supply from Bethlehem Steel, it looked simple. We were involved in distributing oilfield supplies. It had some 80 to 100 people with 21 retail locations and 5 to 6 pipe storage yards. The company required that we stock all products all the time for customers, just like any other business. However, when the demand for oil is high, and drilling activities are frantically busy, you are required to carry more inventory, and when the price falls, you sit with the stock for a long time.

A regular distribution business tends to be of lower profitability. If you cannot sell inventory on a timely basis, the carrying cost becomes prohibitive, and you can be in trouble very fast. Besides, being in commodity type of business, in Bethlehem Supply, steel pipe prices fluctuated wildly. In the 90s oil price hit less than $10 per barrel! Our inventory of $25 million in pipe became worth something like $20 million, five million dollars falling out of the asset value overnight due to the decline in market value of pipe. Also, if you are in a distribution business with many product lines, the chances are that over specific years, you will accumulate so-called residual inventory (6-foot and 10-foot pieces of various size pipes; quarter-pallets, etc.).

As an example, my company Vulcan Rivets and Bolts was in the fastener business. Fasteners tend to have too many sizes of nuts and bolts – hundreds, if not thousands. If we stock ½" bolt in say, a 5,000-unit quantity and an order comes in for 16,000 units, we will probably manufacture 50,000 units. So, if we sell 5,000 units a month, we will carry this inventory for a long time.

Consumer products in distribution businesses is another game altogether. Big box retailers expect you to deliver their products within two days, and if you do not have it in stock, they cancel orders. If you have a big box clientele representing, say, 30% of your total annual revenue, you just cannot effort to lose that customer. If you miss that account, the red ink will be all over the place.

Now online companies, eCommerce businesses, are again game changers. Amazon Worldwide sources products from many tens of thousands (millions?!) of suppliers. You have price pressure and delivery on shelf. Online retailers and brick and mortar retailers are now disrupting each other's businesses. Amazon bought Kohl's and Whole Foods, while Walmart bought online company Flipkart.

Service Businesses:

Service businesses tend not to need/have inventory, machinery or equipment. This part is essential to understand when you are purchasing the business. Asset-rich businesses are more easily financed than service businesses from a lender's perspective as they can place their lien, collateral interest. If there are no assets, usually the lender lends, if it even does, on your cash flow or on a proven track record of operations or other notable financial strengths.

Most of my acquisitions have been in manufacturing and distribution with a few service businesses. Each business has its inherent characteristics.

P. O. BOX 170129

1020 PINSON VALLEY PARKWAY, BIRMINGHAM, ALABAMA 35217

(205) 841-2711

CALL TOLL FREE: IN ALABAMA — 1-800-292-4900 ALL

# Chapter 4: Buying from Large Corporations

Buying a division or subsidiary or even a product line from a large company is different from purchasing an individual owner's business. Large corporations or their subsidiary businesses are usually sold by their employees, a broker, investment bankers, or both.

Most of the time, shareholders/owners are not involved in the transaction; you are dealing with a crucial point-person who is outside hired help. They do not have any emotional involvement in the sale. If the company decides to sell something, they sell it. The package is prepared internally or through outside investment bankers and sent to qualified buyers very systematically with all the bells and whistles.

It was probably a year later in 1985 when I walked in Martin Towers in Bethlehem Pennsylvania at Bethlehem Steel Corporation headquarters. At that time, it was "almighty Bethlehem"! Bethlehem Steel called me after I acquired Vulcan Rivet and Bolt Corporation to discuss buying Buffalo Tank. Buffalo Tank was an underground and aboveground storage tank manufacturer.

I took an early flight from Chicago and walked into their reception area with my little briefcase. After I introduced myself, the receptionist says, "Please, this way, they are waiting for you." They? Hmmm. I thought of John Dresher who was my contact person; perhaps he had someone else with him. It was John Dresher who had sold me Vulcan Rivet and Bolt. The receptionist led me to a large conference room, and to my surprise, there were about a dozen executives formally dressed sitting around! They were surprised that I did not bring my lawyer. I said, no, I thought we were just going to discuss the transaction.

Well, I spent around three hours among all of them, and there were all types of lawyers and executives, EPA representatives and outside investment bankers. After I was through talking, I realized that each one cared only for their little area, such as EPA, Pension, Union, Real Estate, Plants, and on and on. None of them had an all-encompassing view of the business! Each one wanted to protect and address their area of expertise. After that meeting, they were convinced that I was a "genuine buyer". They did not care for anything except getting the deal done. Once a large company makes up its mind to sell and to sell it to you, you have all types of room to improve the agreement. Remember, they have decided to exit that business, and even you if try, many times, to walk away, you cannot!

Another negotiation was also to purchase a business from a large conglomerate. At the last minute, I said that I could not bring $4 million, which was a deficiency in the purchase price. My contact put me on hold on the phone for few minutes and agreed to take $4 million in a non-recourse note (a type of loan secured by collateral).

If you happen to be a second-time buyer after the first-time deal has fallen apart, a deal can get better yet. They for sure do not want egg on their face a second time, nor a third time. In a deal, I had offered and negotiated a price, and this conglomerate decided to sell to someone else for a higher price, and the deal with me fell apart. He called me back some time later and told me that his other deal had fallen apart and was I still interested in buying? Well, it was an opportunity and, I bought that business at one-fourth – 25 cents on the dollar! – of my original offer!


Buying from private individuals, family or small companies:

Buying from a family group or from an individual owner is a whole different ball game. There are lots of emotions and hard negotiations. It is usually not about buying at a bargain, and the chances of the deal falling apart are very high.

To start with, to convince them that you are the right buyer takes forever. Then to overcome their hesitancy about selling or not selling is time-consuming. Many times their whole numerous family is involved, and they may be working in the business that is for sale. The family may be pulling out large salaries and all types of benefits and perquisites. Besides, getting any information from such a group is very difficult.

Buying from large corporations and small individuals or families is 180 degrees apart. Large corporations, once they make up their minds, cannot wait to get rid of the company. While when individuals "want" to sell, it just means they are thinking about it; they just cannot make up their minds; they find all types of reasons not to sell. Their debt, family involvement in the business, emotions – all these play a significant part in the selling process.

Regardless of buying from small owners or large, it is time-consuming to buy a business, with an average deal taking four to six months. In my case, it has taken at the quickest three weeks, and at the longest more than a year.

Buying from large corporations usually provides you with more assets, and the purchase price will be more reasonable. However, it comes with corporate bureaucracy and many corporations' managers have their plan to justify what they are doing in order to get the maximum price for the business.

For example, when I acquired Vulcan Rivets and Bolts from Bethlehem Steel, the bolts and nuts produced by Vulcan (owned by Bethlehem Steel) were given free to Bethlehem when Vulcan purchased the steel to make them from Bethlehem Steel! The manager did not even know how much it cost them to make those nuts and bolts. Making a profit was a far-fetched concept. After I took over, changing that mental attitude and moving into making a profit took forever.

At Buffalo Tank, which I also purchased from Bethlehem Steel, its manager reported to the Bethlehem steel plate production manager. Why?

Tank was a different way for Bethlehem to sell the steel plates it made! Buffalo Tank had no profit motive or even profit accounting. They were just moving Bethlehem Steel's plate production and inventory.

On the other hand, a well-run owner-operated company comes with all the right way of thinking. Usually, they are lean and mean. They do not have large salaries and crowded staff. Most of the people do understand profit and work toward making a profit. A good owner usually runs the company like a cash machine.

When I bought the Aetna Pipe Products, the company ran perfectly. They knew what profit meant, and they always thrived in making money.

Large companies stand behind the buyer after they sell, and if there are any discrepancies, they take care of it. Small company sellers usually do not.

Large companies, especially turnaround companies, usually require less equity; smaller business sellers need more capital.

In small companies, emotions are high and many times, it creates its own type of problems. We had a fixed date for the closing of Aetna Pipe, and closing got delayed by two to three days. When we went for closing, we found out that all accounts payable had been paid up and, in the balance of accounts, payables are next to nothing. Well, the assumption of the accounts payable was supposed to offset and reduce our purchase price. The purchase price due to lower payables came out to be higher! We had a problem: We did not have enough funds to close the deal. We asked the seller, the owner's widow, what happened? She says, "My husband was never late in paying the accounts payable, so I went to the office yesterday and paid them all." How emotional can it be? (We closed with our lender's help; they over-advanced funds to us to cover the shortfall.)

After the day-long closing of Bethlehem Supply, annual revenue $200,000000, I was leaving as a clerk brought 50 additional documents to me and asked me to sign them. I asked, "What are these?" He said they are titles to all the pickup trucks and cars which belong to the company. These assets were not listed. We kept getting real estate coming in to us as late as two years after closing!

On the other hand, if it is a private owner, you usually get whatever is listed and sometimes even less! Many times, an owner may say, "The company has two cars; however, I'd like to keep them. And we also want to keep the cash value of our life insurance," etc.

When buying a high-profile company, the rules are again different. When we were looking at a defense company, the 4X4 truck division of LTV Steel, AM General (sister company of Hummer), the news media was all over the transaction. The military truck division of LTV Steel was high profile; it was an old defense company that had been producing trucks and other vehicles for the US Army since -World War II. We took a run at it when they were shutting down the business. As soon as we started taking interviews of old employees to hire in our new company, local TV stations and large newspapers were at our doorsteps. Senators and congressmen were calling. The seller wanted to protect themselves to avoid any bad publicity about themselves due to shutting down the plant. The more we said, "No comment", the more the media wrote whatever they wanted to write.

Being a defense contractor, we found three significant bottlenecks in financing while buying the business:

First, government accounts receivable are usually not financeable by the traditional asset-based lender (probably because the lender cannot sue the government to collect).

Second, a large Back-to-Back Letter of Credit (two letters of credit to secure financing for a single transaction) is required to get contracts.

Third, when a contractor bills, they also bill part of depreciation, overhead to the government. If the business is in existence, all the equipment and maybe real estate is charged a small percentage to the government every year. Over ten to fifteen years, the full value of the machine and real estate also gets charged to government. Then who owns that equipment? Our lender did not want to finance until LTV Steel warrantied that they owned theirs free and clear. They did not.

By the way, this deal never closed for me. A bid was made with LTV Steel to purchase AM General, army vehicle manufacturer of 4X4 Trucks, sister company of Hummer. Hummer was bought out by a New York company and later by General Motors.

Private individuals, besides getting the selling price, usually want to continue to work at the company they have just sold you. The owner working at the company after selling might be acceptable if the company that you are buying was profitable during his ownership or the owner is transmitting some unique know-how. However, if it is not profitable (or the owner just wants "a job"), keeping the owner after you buy is a huge liability.

# Chapter 5: Leveraged Buy-Outs

A Leveraged BuyOut or LBO is a method in which a buyer finances the purchase by leveraging (using as collateral against a loan) the target company's assets.

Usually, the lender or finance company considers the target company's assets to be anything the company possesses that can be 'turned into cash'. The leverage can be all assets, such as its cash or cash equivalent like its accounts receivable, inventory, building and real estate, machinery and equipment, patents, trademarks, tradename, customer lists and contracts, and everything else that the lender sees of value. The common term for the lender is Blanket Lien which the bank places on the assets until the corresponding loan is paid in full. (A lien prevents you from selling; that way, the bank is sure of having either your cash in loan repayment or to be able to sell the assets to cover it.)

To understand better, I will give an example of a company I owned and bought through a leveraged buyout. I acquired Vulcan Rivets and Bolt in 1985, then a division  of Bethlehem Steel Corporation. Vulcan was in the fastener business, and was started by an individual during the late 1800s to early 1900s. Sometime in mid-1900, Bethlehem Steel acquired that business, and I bought Vulcan from Bethlehem Steel in 1985.

I had minimal cash and no other resources. I approached First Chicago Bank (now Chase Bank) in Chicago to finance it.

Bethlehem Steel was selling Vulcan Rivets and Bolt because it was losing lots of money. Red ink was all over the page every year. At the same time, Bethlehem was so big that this division was too small to pay any attention to fixing.

First, First Chicago Bank looked at the company; profitability was a big problem. I prepared a business plan to explain how I would turn it around and make it profitable. Meanwhile, they looked at the assets of the company, its hard assets. It had reasonably good size plants (around 200,000 square feet), much expensive equipment, a large inventory, and a good size accounts receivable. So, besides my convincing them that my turnaround plan was spot on, they ran their numbers and determined that even if I failed in my turnaround, they could liquidate all the business assets and come out whole.

I bought it. It was a problematic turnaround, but the teams and I did it. I operated it for ten years and sold it off at a good profit.

When you do a leveraged buyout, the bank will look at the company's assets extensively and intensively because that is their insurance to get their lent money back. They will do appraisals of equipment, real estate, the liquidation value of inventory, and all the assets. If the business is losing money, besides all the assets, they will look at the buyer and see his or her track record and history. By that time, I had bought several companies in manufacturing and distribution through a leveraged buyout, so I had a track record.

As you grow and purchase more businesses, it will start becoming a numbers game. With more companies, the chances of having successful business are high!! The success will make it well worth your while. It can bring you hundreds of thousands of dollars or millions of dollars.

When you buy a business, you need to think about the downside risk. If something goes wrong and the business fails, how would you get out with minimum losses? Many companies failed for me, but most of the time, I could get out whole and the number of times I made a profit has made it worthwhile. You can limit your downside risk if you play your cards right.

When I say, 'buying a business', I of course have meant 'buying through financing or leveraging'. Most likely, I'll achieve it through bank financing, and because the bank has financed the transaction, it is indirectly risk-limiting. The bank monitors business performance extremely tightly because the bank has 'skin in the game'. Bank monitoring is proper; it will reduce your risk even if you are sloppy in monitoring business performance. The banks would not let your business down when they themselves risk losing money! There are exceptions, and the bank may lose money, and you may lose your equity. Remember, most of the time, the bank has many times more money sunk in the business than you do with your equity money.

Financing an on-going business is much easier than for a start-up business. Traditional lenders will be a difficult or impossible source of capital for a start-up business because a start-up business does not have any historical data to support past performance. New companies, by nature, do not have many assets that a lender can put their hands on as collateral. An idea, no matter how good it is, is much harder to finance than hard assets.

When you purchase a business, from day one you are in the middle of the action. From that day on, you have full control and the responsibility for the company. All collections that come are yours, and all payables are your responsibility, including payroll.

Payroll or sales and collections don't stop just because you are a new owner! Many times, I compare purchasing a good on-going business as an inheritance. When the owner of a business retires and turns it over to his son or daughter, the son or daughter becomes the owner and enjoys the fruits of their father's years of hard work! When you buy a business, the owner goes away, almost like father turned over business to you. Sure, there will be a bank watching over your shoulder. The lender does not make any business decisions for you or take any benefit except agreed-upon loan payment. They will try to protect their loans by monitoring your business periodically. More power to them, they have the same interest as you in operating a business profitably. You get a second experienced eye at almost no cost.

My first experience of leveraging came when I worked for Union Carbide as an engineer, but it was not with my first business purchase. My leveraging experiences all started when I lived in a second-floor apartment of a two-story building. The landlord was a factory worker who worked all his life and saved enough money to purchase the two-flat building. He lived on the first floor, and unfortunately, I was his first tenant on the second floor. He bothered me for everything. If my one-year-old daughter cried, he complained. When it snowed in Chicago, he insisted we use a dangerous rear porch. With his ongoing complaints, I got tired and purchased a twelve-flat apartment building in 1974 for $80,000 with a $10,000 down payment (all a lot of money in 1964, but look at it this way: a single family home in the Midwest was running an average of $30,000 in those days) that was seller-financed. At the closing, prorating real estate taxes, which are one year behind in Illinois, prorating security deposit, and advanced rent paid, the down payment got reduced from $10,000 to less than $5,000. With a 5% investment, I leveraged 95% against the assets (the real estate – the building itself), which I did not own!! I moved in, and from day one, I had a positive cash flow.

It was a great lesson on leveraging ... and how to deal with a cranky landlord! There was very little down payment; it was seller-financed. I had a free apartment and all the depreciation! After that, I purchased several buildings and made good money on them until the early 1980s.

Unless you purchase at a low purchase price, the property business is most likely cash-flow-poor. Your income (rents) can barely support the mortgage and expenses. You most probably have a negative cash flow. You make money mostly when you sell the property.

Existing businesses – manufacturing, and others – are different from a real estate business. Businesses possess a lot more collateral (aka hard assets) for financing and (usually) excellent cash flow.

The business you purchase may have real estate to leverage; it has machinery and equipment to leverage; it has the inventory to leverage; and best of all, accounts receivable to leverage! Many times the cash already in the company comes with it, which offsets your cash equity portion directly.

I experienced all this first time when I purchased my first company, Aetna Pipe Products of Illinois. At the time, I had sold an apartment building, and I made $80,000 which was available to me to invest. I purchased Aetna Pipe Products merely because I just wanted to go into my own business.

It was a pleasant surprise! The company business was sixty years old and did $2 million a year in sales volume. From day one, I was selling and shipping between $8,000-$9,000 worth of goods per day.

I financed 80% toward receivables, and 50% towards inventory. I also funded term debt against machinery and real estate. The financing was great. I could buy a business, which had a $2 million volume for $85,000 of my own money.

NOTE: The size of the numbers change over the years due to inflation, but the proportions should be the same!

Asset Based Lending:

I understand that a person named Walter Heller initially pioneered asset-based lending. Since then, after many years of experience, lenders incorporated another part of leveraging such as inventories, machinery and equipment, and real estate. This way, asset-based lenders have perfected the lending system and have made a fine-tuned scientific formula out of it.

As its name indicates, pure asset-based lending lends only on assets and on a percentage advance basis, strictly governed by assets and their value. When the company is liquidated, the lender is able to get his money out through sale of the assets. The formula is self-correcting and, if used correctly, is risk-free for the lender. All asset-based lenders monitor loans weekly once the transaction completed. I found this to be one of the better ways to purchase companies while at the same time taking the risk out for the lender and owner.

When you buy a company through a leveraged buyout, you are leveraging assets of the target company through an asset-based lender. Many times, a company may not have enough assets to support the buyout, but it may help the higher purchase price from cash flow. In that case, the lender may lend more money than the assets actually support. Several firms may invest with you in purchasing a company if they are comfortable with you; however, for a first-time buyer it is hard, and in the future, once you have a successful company, you may not even need them.

When you are analyzing a target company for acquisition and planning for asset-based financing, you should analyze the business with the buyer's eye but also through the lender's eye.

As a buyer, you may be emotional because you may want to buy the business. You may like the product line. Your wife's brother may say that "it's a great company, so buy already"!" You might be working for the company's competition – and many more emotion-based scenarios. Don't get married to an idea. Be analytical! Don't forget the bank does not have any emotional reasons – none at all – to finance you. Bankers are more practical, down to earth, business analyzers (keeping exceptional cases out). They want to protect the money they lend and will consider the worst scenario. If they are uncomfortable about their loan being repaid, chances are you will not get financing!

In a real sense, the buyer should respect the lender's opinion and experience. His concern about getting his loan paid back must be your prime concern also! You don't want to purchase a business that may fail; neither does the lender want to lend you money for a business which may fail!

Let us go to an example of a specific purchase.

You come across a business that is available for sale. It looks reasonable, and you want to explore it. If it has a professional middleman (broker, investment banker, accounting firm, internal sales division), it is easier to get information than directly from the owner. Ultimately, the information you need will come from the seller and the target company, but usually, the owner/seller (as opposed to the corporate seller) is more emotional about his business. To pursue further, you should ask the seller the list of items described further in the "Due-Diligence" section of this book.

There is a big list of information you will need to sift through. The list will vary a bit from one type of business to another, but the core information will be similar.

Once you receive some of this information, you may start going through item by item. Analyze it all yourself first. Naturally, you look at the product line first. Usually, you should keep your mind open about the product line until you review the profitability of the business.

At this stage, do not spend a lot of time becoming a product expert. Move on to look at the financial statement; review the profit and loss statement. Some who read this book may say to themselves that they do not know about financial statements. Well, you may want to learn it if you want to be independent in your analysis of potential businesses to buy; in all cases, it will be essential to understand the "basics of business numbers". You will be able to use this knowhow time after time. I am not saying you should be an expert, but you can learn by flipping through the pages, and understand profit/loss, and asset/liability, etc. If you are determined to go into business, the foundation and reason for doing so is money and wealth, and you had better learn the numbers that express that. Spend the time. Believe me, it is worth it.

A main reason for business failure is that the owner or CEO is not 'following the money'. You can have a great product line and a profitable product line, but if you are not aware of the money flows, it can be a disastrous situation.

# Chapter 6: Buying Out of Bankruptcy

Buying a business out of bankruptcy is a unique experience.

Over the years, bankruptcy laws have changed. If a company is in bankruptcy, it is primarily that the business is facing multiple issues detrimental to its ongoing business operations. The company may have more debt than assets; it may no longer have the necessary funds to operate the business; the business might have shut down a previously key product line due to a lack of demand for it now. It may have suffered an employee strike; the lender might have pulled the loan; unsecured creditors may have pushed the business into bankruptcy; a substantial lawsuit might have been filed against it (and cost a lot of the business's cash in legal fees…). And so on and on.

Once the business is found insolvent, the company files for bankruptcy, which is Chapter 7 (according to US Federal Bankruptcy Law). Once it is in Chapter 7, the company shuts down and no business is supposed to be conducted. The filings are done in the Federal bankruptcy court. If the owner believes that if given time, the company can be saved, then the owner converts the Chapter 7 into what is called Chapter 11. Under the Chapter 11 provision, the company continues to operate under bankruptcy code guidelines. Bankruptcy codes and information are very complex legal laws, so one should contact a bankruptcy lawyer, consult and learn.

When a business files Chapter 7 and does not convert into Chapter 11, most if not all of the assets become available to be liquidated. Liquidation is conducted under the supervision of a bankruptcy trustee.

If it is converted into Chapter 11, the business gets breathing room to be reorganized, liquidated, or sold, also under the law of bankruptcy. Upon the filing of Chapter 11, most of the past payables get frozen, and business can continue operating. The court gives industry-specific leeway to run the business, depending upon what the business requires to maintain activities. Once in Chapter 11, the company has a few choices – primarily to continue operating as it reorganizes, or to sell the company. The sale can offer only a part of business or the whole of it. It will go to the highest bidder. This type of sale is called Section 363 Sale under the Federal bankruptcy code.

If you'd like to acquire the business under this provision of Section 363 sale, you need to approach the bankruptcy trustee or the company's bankruptcy attorney. They will usually provide you with a confidentiality agreement to be signed and then share information about the company. Once you receive information, you must do a lot more due diligence (your comprehensive examination of the company, its assets and liabilities and potential in the markets) on your own to see if you want to buy it, and if the company is worth buying.

Because the company is in bankruptcy and insolvent, you should expect that the business has significant problems, whether it is losses, lawsuits, outdated/unsaleable products, or other circumstances against it. Unlike a standard buyout, this type of business becomes difficult to investigate because, usually, the seller/owner is not there.

Once you decide you like the business and you want to buy it, you should discuss it with the bankruptcy trustee or the company's bankruptcy attorney. It can be a Letter of Intent that you submit, or they may give you their Purchase and Sale Contract to bid on. It gets sold to the buyer making the highest and best offer.

# Chapter 7: Selecting Lenders & Lender Mindset

Vulcan Rivet and Bolt was my second purchased company. I was all excited as it was five times bigger than my first company. I went to First Chicago Bank because a banker who was at Cole Taylor Bank and financed my Aetna Pipe Products now had moved to First Chicago Bank. In talking, he introduced me to First Chicago, and First Chicago financed my Vulcan buyout. It was, if I recall correctly, a $5 million line of credit, and the outstanding loan was about $4 million. I do not remember, but I think I put small equity (remember that 'equity' here means 'my own cash') of no more than 10%, and First Chicago financed the remainder. Financing was typical asset-based lending where they financed 80% of receivables, 50% of good inventory, machinery/equipment and the real estate.

After the buyout, I started operating the company. The business was losing money, and I began reducing expenses by automating some of the production lines and reducing headcounts. In about four months or so, I found out that it was not working. One of the product lines of the company was Railroad Spikes. It was a loser. The more we produced, the more we lost.

I was frustrated, and it just was not working. However, the bank was fine. It had all the assets, and they were not that much concerned. One day I went to the plant in Birmingham, and my manager broke the news that we lost Union Pacific Railroad company's business. Almost $2 million in annual revenues was gone. As it was not making money and now the loss of this size of the volume, I did not know what I would do.

The next day I received a phone call out of nowhere. He introduced himself and asked me if I wanted to sell the Railroad Spike business. I felt like the phone call came from heaven. I kept a straight face, and after negotiations, I sold the complete line for $650,000 – a product line which I had bought for less than $50,000! Within a month they paid all $650,000 and on top of it, I sold all the inventory for additional cash and collected all the receivables for even more cash. Wow! Great deal! I netted almost $1,500,000 in cash. I was very proud of myself. Not only had I sold a losing business, but I paid down the substantial loans of First Chicago!

Well, the plot thickens as they say. I did not know the bank's mindset. I got a phone call from First Chicago informing me that they would not finance me anymore and that I needed to move the loan. "Why?", I ask. They said that I was too small, my loan balance was 'only' $2,500,000, and their minimum loan was $4,000,000! They kicked me out because I had paid down the loan!

As was well though, when I went to a smaller bank, Exchange National Bank. They financed Vulcan and subsequently Exchange National Bank got bought out by LaSalle Bank.

This was a great lesson. What is it this lesson? Simply that all banks work differently; banks have different goals and 'personalities'. They have different niches. When you go to get financed, look for a matching bank. Ask all types of questions. Ask other business people, even other bankers. If Leveraged Buyouts are not their game, you will waste lots of time talking to them, only to find they will not fund. The worst thing is if they fund without knowing how asset-based lending, collateral, and borrowing work, they will very soon get frustrated and put you in default.

Some banks are community/small business lenders. They do not have the backroom expertise to monitor loans. Once they give credit, usually, they do not look at you so long as you continue to pay the debt service. While a correct asset-based lender will monitor you almost every day, they know it, and in a difficult time, they will work with you.

I have had banks financing me for all types of companies. After so many deals, I have concluded that each bank kind of develops its own culture, character and niches. You'd better know what those are if you expect them to lend to you!

# Chapter 8: Types of Businesses & Profitability

There are all types of businesses: manufacturing, service, distribution, pharmaceutical, and many more. However, all companies have some common goals: to make a juicy profit, consistently year after year. All owners have a common goal, too: to make a good, consistent living for themselves from the business. If you are going to own one or more businesses, you want the one(s) you will own to be profitable!

So, when you are buying, making sure that it is profitable or can be made to be profitable. That is very important. As we said before, if you cannot make it productive, it will die. Are you always sure that it would become profitable? Not necessarily, even with a great turnaround plan. There will always be a risk, and you should take the risk. However, if you conclude that it can be not made to be quickly productive (and how to achieve that), do not buy it. At the same time, if you need 100% assurance of owning a 'winning' business, move on – there is no such guarantee. The chances that you will buy a business at all are little or none if you 'need to be 100% sure' before buying.

In the 'olden' (pre-internet) days, we were 100% dependent on the seller's mercy to find out any information about his business. Unless he gave you the data and answers you wanted/needed, you just could not get it. Times have changed. There are many publicly available avenues through which you can get information. Almost all the businesses have websites, appear in independent review sites. Get as much information online and offline as you can. Go to stores, distributors, competitors, and study the products or services. Get catalogs. In other words, do full and proper research – due diligence – of that business. There are all types of information available on the internet without paying any money.

The next step after getting the information or cursory information from outside sources would be to get information from seller. The seller will generally give you all the information you need if he or she is convinced that you are a genuine and capable buyer. Yet most of the time, it is a very involved but delicate process to get a full package. If it is an institutional seller like an investment bank, the qualification will be straightforward, such as the financial strength of the buyer. However, if it is a private seller, depending on the seller's experience and background, a request for information needs to be handled tactfully.

Once you get the package (again, that is the seller's or seller's representatives packet of information about the company for sale), review it. Please do not run to advisors instantly because it usually costs money. Even if it does not cost money (say it's a friend or relative), do not go to them, because their reviews will be colored by their own background and opinions. The first thing to do, once you get the package, is to read it, study it, and spend all the time you need on it – yourself. Even if you do not fully understand, try to read it through. Review the whole package of information. Also, even if you are not an accountant, review the financial statement. You may be surprised how many things you can figure out. Remember, it is for you that you are buying the business, and it is you who must live with it once you buy it. It is you who must later also 'follow the money'.

Write up questions of items that you do not understand. Do not feel bad asking those and as many other questions as you have to the seller or seller's agent. A motivated seller is always happy to see a genuine buyer. Do not feel bad asking questions about the industry or their expertise. If seller is also the owner, he or she is a wealth of information. They are usually very good at what they are doing. Many new buyers typically assume that the seller is not knowledgeable and may be old, inherited the business, or is just not qualified. That is usually mistaken. My experience says that most of the owner/sellers are very smart. Wherever they say that, "This cannot be done", listen carefully.

For example, your plan may 'prove' that you can increase business by 5%, and he may say, "No, you cannot improve it because of … [this and that reason]." Listen to him or her. He is generally right, and without asking, you would find it out anyway after you buy it. If he says that, "We went to the Mexican market and lost because of … [this]," usually he is right.

The wealth of information a seller brings to you is priceless. Use it, and genuinely appreciate it. Make a note of it and continue the dialogue. All the seller wants is for the buyer to be successful and for the business to continue to prosper once he sells it or is gone. Most of the time, they have a vested interest in an ongoing business. They might have taken a note or maybe have a contract to work in the business after the sale to you, or perhaps some of his friends/family are working in the business. Almost all have a high desire that you maintain the employees. So, in a way, the seller has a very high degree of interest in making sure that:

- He sells it successfully with the best price

- The business continues operating

- Most of the employees remain employed

- He keeps getting paid on his note if he takes a note back

- Continues to get paid on earnout if there is any

- Continues to get the rent paid if he retains ownership of the building

- The company survives, and he remains friendly with the buyer And on and on.

Also, remember, once the business is sold and becomes successful, his liabilities related to misrepresentation, adjustments, and so on decline drastically. A successful, financially profitable business when sold and continuing to operate, has fewer litigations between buyer and seller.

I always have tried to have a continued good relationship with active sellers. They bring credibility to the business and offer a smooth transition. Usually, you can work out a transition agreement with him for the first three months or so at no or little cost. I like to have a good relationship with him for a long time so that I can use him as a sounding board. Good Relationships are Priceless in the Business of Buying Businesses!

Now, for all the above, we are generally talking about active, operating sellers and not an absentee sellers or agents. They are different.

Once you study the information package thoroughly, you need to sit down with the seller as many times as you need to get it and get many bright ideas. Besides what he describes, insist on on-site visits, office visits, sample products, evaluations, etc.

As for site visits, most of the time, the seller may not want to meet you at first in your early talks at the place of business, because he usually does not wish for anyone (especially employees) to find out that the business is for sale. He may meet you at a restaurant or your office or somewhere else. You should do that.

When you see the seller is the time to score points with him to show that you are a genuine buyer. If he does not get that warm, fuzzy feeling about you, it will be an uphill battle. You may get shut out entirely. During this meeting, you also should learn many things about him and his business. For example, you might have heard that the reason he is selling is due to his health, or that he is retiring. Also, if you see him as a 40 year old healthy person, something is wrong...! Or he may be driving a Mercedes and have expensive taste, you know that he may be drawing a big salary from the business or that this business is not his primary livelihood. Also, you would know how friendly he or she is. He may have one of his employees as advisor who can also be helpful. So, this first meeting is a significant opportunity to find out more about the seller. If it is an institutional seller, you would have more upfront qualifying meetings with both parties that flow in a more straightforward manner.

After this goes well comes a site or business visit. You want to touch and feel the business. When I say business, I mean everything: Look at and ask about product, plant, office, environment, employees, everything. Once you go there, a visit is priceless for collecting information.

Once you see the product, it will say many things. Let us say you went to acquire a company which makes bar soap. Instantly, you would either recognize the product as a brand or not accept the product. Now, you would also remember the financial statements, and you should be able to associate more with cost, etc. You would even know how many SKUs they have. If they have 200 SKUs of products and are doing $2,000,000 volume, you know now that there are too many SKUs. Or if there are only two types of bar soap in the product line, you know that there are more manageable SKUs. While walking around their place of business, you will see if they have a plant or not, that is, if they are getting product made outside or inhouse.

# Chapter 9: Sale of Business Package, Offering Memorandum

The seller or seller's agent usually prepares a business package – that valuable packet of information about the business for sale. Once the buyer signs a confidentiality agreement, the seller or seller's agent sends the business package. The buyer reviews it and makes his decision to go further toward a purchase or pass on it.

The package usually contains a full description of the business, and details the performance of business in the form of financial statements of past, present, and projected future. Brochures and catalogs describe the product lines of the business. The package, due to limitations of the size of the package, usually contains a summary or internally generated numbers. Audited statements, appraisal of real estate, appraisal of machinery and equipment, EPA report, union contract, etc. are not included. If the buyer does want to proceed, he goes in a detailed study of all those areas. If it is a larger company and represented by a broker or other agent, a so-called 'data room' is put together. This data room holds all the above information and many more items, such as inventory detail, costing, past historical financial statements, advertising, material sale, and marketing network.

As I have said, Information Is King Before You Buy! (Which is why I have already told you several times, to find things out in detail – and to understand the information you are looking at!)

Now, this does not mean that seller and the package are always aboveboard. Many times, they do present a better picture than reality. They dress it up and do so-called add-backs. Add-backs are usually one-time expenses, seller's compensation, depreciation, capital expenditure, and similar things. They do try to put more items in those areas, so the bottom-line profit looks more better than it is.

For example, say the owner is drawing $250,000 in 'expenses', and he adds it back to the bottom line as 'seller's compensation'. You should study carefully and ask yourself, "Is this person active in the business? If he is, would you need another person at that place when he leaves? If you do, how much would it cost? The capital expenses, if he is adding up, are this non-recurring?" Many times equipment, such as molds, dies or types of specialist equipment need replacing every year. Many times, high tech computers and other state-of-the-art equipment get outdated in a year or two. If this is the case, it is a reasonable expense and not a capital expense. These types of items should not be added as profit.

Many owners give you numbers on a spreadsheet. You should ask them for actual financial statements and not just numbers on the worksheet.

Audited accounts are always better if the company gets prepared tax returns; if not included, the owner should provide them to you.

You will be surprised if you go into the detail of how many small expenses are logged in for an ongoing business.

# Chapter 10: Visiting a Place of Business & Meeting Owners

Most of the time as I have said, a seller may not want to meet you at the site of business right away because he usually does not want anyone working there to find out that business is for sale. You should understand and acknowledge this sensitivity; otherwise it might put the whole negotiation in jeopardy. This is the time to know him to show that you are a genuine buyer. You don't want him to shut you out; you really need him to give you information!

During this and successive meetings, learn as much as you can about him and his business, just through normal conversation. For example ... Why is he selling? Is it an Exit Strategy that he is implementing? Is this his only business? Do his family members still work in the business? What have been the most notable ups and most disastrous downs of the business and the industry?

Make sure you ask for his business card when the session is complete. If he gives his business card of the company he is selling, it may have the address of the business, phone numbers, and a website and email address. If he gives you a card from a different company, it also may give you his strength and weakness of other ventures where he is involved.

If the company is in bankruptcy or an assignee sale, usually a consultant is there to sell the business. Depending on the company, many times, the previous owner would also be there. If you are meeting the consultant or trustee, it is advisable to ask him to bring the owner as well. The owner knows much more about the business than a short-term consultant. Also, this way, you will understand what the owner's interest is and be able to connect to those interests and perhaps obtain even more information of value. Usually, he has lost everything due to bankruptcy (not just his business perhaps), or he foresees that he will be losing everything if things keep going as they have. He can be a key person to continue operations after you acquire it, so you need to find out if indeed he has the required skills, knowledge and experience – and desire.

If it is an institutional seller, you will be contacted by a divestiture manager or an agent of the company. They also by then would have done some preliminary pre-qualification of you.

When I was buying the company from Bethlehem Steel, one of their business development people who oversaw the sale took a trip to Chicago, to my place of business. He did not tell me. However, later, he said that he drove by and did some discovery about me and my business. In other words?

Site and owner visits go both ways! They want to know about you as much as you want to know about them.

When you meet, you will have a more organized meeting with the broker and company manager. It will be a more qualifying meeting by both parties.

After this initial contact and meeting comes a site or business visit. You want to touch and feel the business: Put your eyes on everything! Once you are there, the additional types of information you can collect are as or more important than those catalogs and packages which you saw before. Information Is King! (Or have I mentioned this?)

Every visit will be a unique visit. You will learn a lot. When I visited a company that I assumed to be small and troubled, I found that it was massive (and I never would have imagined the scope without being there personally – and that is why site visits are vital. You can miss the obvious when studying documentation. You cannot miss it when it is spread before your eyes). It is the one that made those 4X4 trucks for military and huge equipment that I told you about in Chapter 4. The plant alone was one million square feet under one roof and on 400 acres of land with a long driveway. The presentation room, as they explained to us, was huge and laid out like a war strategic planning room. Upon a push of a button, a wall would move, and the screen would show up! I was not prepared for this type and size of business. In a company which was losing money, if I start operating a one million square foot plant without a profits – if nothing else, the utility bills and real estate taxes alone will put me out of business! So my visit was absolutely eye opening and highly beneficial.

At the end of the meeting I had (see Chapter 4) with that wide range of specialists (attorney, EPA rep, company rep, etc.), as I was coming home in the plane, I realized, "Price?! What I am saying is so insignificant that it does not matter. They just want to get rid of business as an ongoing business, so it does not come back to them." The site visit and the meeting and long talks with all the interested, informed parties was crucial to this decision of mine: Upon my return, I adjusted my price well downward and also asked the seller to take a second-position subordinated note. I bought that business at a lower price, with subordinated seller financing and most of the rest was borrowed money from the bank. Moral of the story: Any and all personal site visits and face-to-face talks with the seller and his representatives are well worth the energy and time spent by the buyer. And might just be worth millions of dollars that you never have to commit to it!

# Chapter 11:
# Confidentiality Agreement

All most all sellers or seller's agents will ask you to sign a Confidentiality Agreement before they release any information. Confidentiality varies from one format to another. It is a legal binding agreement so it is important to read and understand the document.

Primarily it is designed so that a potential buyer cannot use the information provided for any other reason except to acquire the company. Usually, it has covenants (agreements) that prohibit the information from being disclosed to anyone else except for yourself and the representative who assists you. Some of them also insist that people who review the document also sign them. They vary from simple one-page documents to multiple pages.

If you are uncomfortable, it is not a bad idea to have it reviewed by a lawyer. I usually read it carefully, and if something is not acceptable, I bring it to the seller or seller's agent and have them modify that clause or section.

The confidentiality agreements for a private company and a public company also have differences.

<u>Private Company Confidentiality Agreement:</u>

It has general provisions, as described above. When you receive a confidentiality agreement, review and get yourself familiar with it. There is no standard; it varies in language and content. It usually comes from a broker or owner of the business. Once you sign, they will countersign and send you one original back.

The confidentiality agreement also has a provision where, for a given multiple of years, you can not disclose the information or use the information if you do not buy the business.

It also usually restrains you from contacting any of the employees or hiring any of the employees. Visiting the place of business is also forbidden unless accompanied by seller or seller's agent.

If you do violate the agreement, the damage clause is usually substantial. Regardless, as you are bound by the contract, it is a good business practice to keep the information in strict confidence and follow the agreement requirements. All the information provided by them must also be returned to them, including copies and worksheets made for that business.

<u>Public Company Confidentiality Agreement:</u>

The SEC regulates public companies (these are companies listed and traded on the stock exchanges). Besides all the private companies' provisions, a public company has a rule where you are restricted from buying and selling its shares. The information you get, including projections, is considered 'insider information', so you cannot play with their security while you are bound by the confidentiality agreement.

It also applies to your advisors, consultants, and family members – whoever has that information. If you own shares of that company, you should disclose it to the public company. Many times, if you own a small number of shares, it is easier to sell before you receive any information; that way, you are not stuck for a few years and unable to sell the shares.

# Chapter 12: Due Diligence Package & Request

Once you sign the confidentiality agreement, a package or offering memorandum arrives. Sometimes it is a loosely assembled set of documents, financial and other information. Sometimes it is a polished and professionally rendered informative book about the business. Most of the time, however, you receive something in between.

A well assembled package has the following sections/information. If it does not, the buyer should request whatever is missing and applicable to the type of business for sale.

- Description of business for sale and selling price
- History, current condition, and market
- Sales channels
- Website information
- Product catalogs and description
- Financials such as:
    - Income Statement
    - Balance Sheet

- Cash Flow Statement

- Re-Cast Financial Statement

- Audited Financial Statements for three years

- Appraisals Building or lease

- Appraisals of machinery and equipment

- Formal or informal appraisal of real estate

- Inventory

  - Finished

  - Raw

  - Work in process

  - Turn of inventory

- Estimated liquidation value on products inventory

- Accounts receivable and aging

- Accounts payable and aging

- History of the company's business

- Product line and market

- Any patents, trademark, long term contracts, etc.

It also may include some additional specifics related to the business, such as licensing agreements, patents, trademarks, deeds, other tangible and intangible assets. This may sound like a big list. Well – it is! It is extremely important that you get this information (and more depending on the specific industry). Generally, this list is sufficient for most companies you will look at.

An excellent package is a wealth of information. You need to digest all of it, and whatever more you need, you need to request. Many sellers do not provide some types of information (such as a customer list or a vendor list) until you enter into a purchase and sale agreement.

Information of this nature tends to be massive, so many times – rather than getting it at your address – you go to the seller's designated place(a Data Room) and get all the information analyzed.

Once you have this information, start going through it item by item. Analyze it yourself first and put aside the pieces you need further advice about from accountants or attorneys. Again, if you are determined to own or operate any type of business, I strongly advise you to get lessons or training in 'business math' and 'how to read financial statements'. It provides peace of mind when considering different businesses that are for sale.

You must study the current numbers, but you also look at the past numbers and at the industry's numbers. The business may be declining, so ask why: Is it due to a greater economic situation (recession; COVID-19 shutdown; major industry in the area closed, etc.)? The company may be growing, and you should also attempt to understand why: Is it due to baby boomer product or service demand in this industry? Or is it a cyclical industry experiencing a 'bubble' such as construction, even seasonal? You want to know the information so you can be an intelligent buyer in projecting the future state of the business after you buy it. Surprises will not

... surprise you as much when you have asked the deep questions and studied both the company and the industry data. A huge benefit of this curiosity: You do not overpay for the business.

Understanding the liability side of the business is as important as itemizing and valuing its assets. EPA liability can be huge, and a pension liability of a company can be lingering on for an extended time (if a pensioned employee retires at age 70 and lives to collect his pension through age 97, that is 27 years of payments and record-keeping for the business – just as an example). These are government-regulated areas, and if the business has those issues, you should seek appropriate advice. Some of the pension liability can be a personal liability, regardless of the company being a corporation.

If a company has a labor union (a Bargaining Unit), you must study the contract and seek professional advice. The labor union can have successor liability; or a contract may be expiring at/near the time of changing ownership. The work rule, seniority rule, and many other provisions in a union contract must be analyzed from a specialist business and legal perspective. A specific type of service requires union labor only. The owner can give you that information.

Suppliers and vendors (the business's supply chain) should be reviewed carefully. The current owner may well have been in business for a long time and have a good relationship with suppliers; he may have had such long relationships that he has never ever renegotiated terms of those contracts! You will not know unless you read and ask. You may not get the same terms that he is getting. In other words, he may be paying in 45 days, and you may have to pay in 30 days or 15 days. Even worst, a supplier may ask you to pay cash on delivery or advance payment. Supplier's credit terms impact your cash need of business to run.

If you are importing product from overseas as all or part of business operations, you may need to open a Letter of Credit. A letter of credit may require additional cash because the existing letter of credit of the seller will be extinguished when a sale closes.

If you know all these areas of operation and administration in advance, you can negotiate with the seller to help you, such as giving you time to research and negotiate with current or new vendors, providers and suppliers.

As examples of how I have dealt with such matters, when we bought businesses from steel companies, we negotiated longer credit terms from them, which helped us with cash flow. In other companies, we asked for the seller's Letter of Credit to be continued for one year, so we did not have to renegotiate one for a year. While negotiating a union contract, we arranged for a new defined contribution plan (401K) and did not assume the defined benefit plan of the seller. In this case, we confined our responsibility for pension liability. We also negotiated health benefits ahead of time (before we bought the company).

Payroll and payroll taxes, if not paid current, become the owner's liability. One must investigate how they are/were paid. All accrued vacations shall be defined and agreed to be paid at closing to those employees (or the seller gives credit to the buyer for the amounts at closing).

If there is any litigation, you should seek the advice of a lawyer to analyze the contexts and circumstances.

# Chapter 13: Steps of Buying a Business

Letter of Intent (LOI)

Once you like the business and you decide to buy it, the first step is sending a Letter of Intent or LOI.

A Letter of Intent spells out your intention to buy the business. It may say only that you are interested in purchasing the company, or it may describe many more details such as price, date of closing, terms, and conditions of buying. Most LOI are written in simple, everyday business language. Sometimes people may also send letters of interest. Varieties of letter of intent can be found on the internet, including on-web base legal sites. You may use them if you are comfortable, or you may seek an attorney's advice and have it written for you. You are a businessman, and you must tell the attorney what price, when, and with what terms and conditions you might be interested in buying the business.

This letter of interest or letter of intent is legally binding if it specifically states that it is; otherwise it is not binding. You can also make offers verbally and can get feedback from the seller to discover if his price and terms are in the range of what you are offering.

Purchase and Sale Agreement

Once the letter of intent is submitted, and the seller agrees to sell and the buyer agrees to buy, the second document you need is the Purchase and Sale Agreement. This document is very detailed and usually prepared by an attorney. Depending on the business you are buying, it spells out many details such as:

- The company you are buying, name, and type of corporate entity.

- Asset sale or stock sale or combination of both.

- Purchase price you are paying: with details of how, such as cash, note, financing and/or time.

- List of assets you are buying: business name, entity, asset sale or stock sale, real estate if any, machinery and equipment, jigs and fixtures, tangible assets such as cash in the company, accounts receivable, notes, royalties, intellectual property, patents, trademarks, phone numbers, fax numbers, domain names, websites, vehicles, and other assets.

- Liabilities you are assuming: loans, debt, accounts payable, payroll, employee vacation pay, pension liability, product liability, pending litigation, union liability if any, etc.

- Employees at closing: headcount, payroll, vacations, insurance policy coverage, benefits – and placing them under the buying entity's payroll from day one.
- Union/Bargaining Unit details: pension plan, 401 K plan, company policy, etc.
- Closing date time and place: wire transfer instructions to pay the purchase price or in detail how the purchase price will be paid, when warranty and representations by seller and buyer related to business and information are given.
- Confidentiality of transaction, press releases, if any.

### Financing, Loan and Security Agreement

Using my approach, you will be borrowing money to buy a business either from a lender, venture capitalists, your friends and relatives, the seller, and other resources. All those who are lending the funds will have documents associated with it detailing how you and your buying entity will pay the loan back: how much you are borrowing, when you start paying, the interest rate, the covenants you must observe for business performance, etc. All those are spelled out by the lender. It is usually called a Loan and Security Agreement.

The lender many times verifies the assets on which it is lending by getting the appraisal done on assets such as real estate, inventory, machinery equipment, and accounts receivable.

If there is more than one lender, they will have priority on security and subordination agreements. The lender often provides this document, and you should study that it reflects what you can commit to and that you understand it. The buyer and the bank's lawyer typically get involved in this document and agree.

# Chapter 14: Closing to Buy the Business

You are ready to 'close'. Closing is just that – closing the deal, signing all the paperwork, paying the buy-price to own the business, wrapping it all up so that you now fully own the business. At that time, the company changes hands: the buyer receives a business in ownership and its seller gives up the business to that new owner.

At the pre-agreed date, all the documents as defined in the Purchase and Sale Agreement are gathered, all the funds are kept ready, all the promissory notes are drafted, all the authorized signatures affixed, the wire transfer is effected, the buyer pays the seller directly or through his bank.

To arrive at the time of closing, buyer and seller worked hard for weeks and months, sometimes even years, and the day has come. Besides all the above documents, the buyer should think about the practicalities of taking over the business operations and administration.

When you buy a business, and just before closing, you should make a punch list of what you would need or need to do as soon as you buy. Here are a few critical topics to think of and be prepared for:

- New business name, registration in the state, county city, etc.

- FEIN Number. Federal Tax Identification Number, which is given to all the businesses which are registered to operate a business in a US state. The buyer will have to apply for it a few days in advance.

- Opening bank accounts and having checks, deposit slips produced; getting authorized individuals' signatures on file. Bank account security, user ID, passwords, etc.

- Decision about hiring only some or all of the seller's employees.

- Employee transfer applications, if you are getting all those employees who worked for the seller or the seller's business. Their applications shall have all their information such as name, address, phone number, social security number, and all existing resumes, payroll records, vacation records, etc. Payroll period and transfer paycheck, hard-soft, or direct deposit.

- Pension and 401K, if any, and all related documents and records.

- Utility transfers such as electric, gas and other fuel, water, phone system, website domain hosting, etc.

- All intellectual property (IP) transfer, such as patents, trademarks, copyrights, websites and names of the business.

- All vehicle title/deed transfers, if any.

- All lease agreements if you are accepting to take them over and deeds of ownership, on items such as real estate, vehicles, computer and office equipment, plant machinery, and equipment.

- The precise cut-off date for checks received and payables paid (such as midnight of the date of closing, before or after).

- After closing, if the seller's checks keep coming and bills keep coming, where to send them.

- If product returns come from the past business and credit has to be issued, how and when and who pays.

- If a product carries a warranty, the cost of servicing the warranty (who pays and how much).

- All the insurance policies: general and commercial asset and liability coverage, workman's compensation insurance, vehicle and real estate insurance, fraud protection, officers and directors liability insurance (as well as group life insurance for staff, as applicable in their benefits packages).

I am sure there are more items for some types of businesses, just as there are a few which will not apply to your newly purchased business.

# Chapter 15: Buying Business with…

I have mentioned how to fund your new purchase throughout these pages with numerous examples from my own experience. Let us break it down again into the four 'types' of money that can help you pay for that newly acquired business.

*Buying a Business with Little Money*

You have little ready cash of your own – little, in relation to a business's sale price. Or you have more money than needed, but don't want to put it all on this one deal.

This type of business purchase is funded with a small equity (a small amount of your own money) and most of the remaining money is borrowed from a lender or injected by another type of investor.

Most of the time, the lender is a bank or financial institute, sometimes a private party, or a venture capitalist. Consider that even the seller can bring money to the table to help you buy his business.

If you borrow funds from traditional lenders, the lender will look at the *assets and underlying collateral as security* of the lender's loan, as discussed.

If the lender is comfortable with the collateral securing the loan, and the company's cash flow supports the lender's debt repayment, you may be able to buy a business with anywhere from five percent to twenty percent down payment. What little money you want to put in is on you, and you must work at it.

Let us review and do an exercise about the underlying assets that the lender will look to lend. The lender will look at good accounts receivable and may lend you as much as 80% of the outstanding accounts receivable amount.

As an example of a business, take a company doing $2 Million a year in revenue. Its standard credit term is 30 days net. The receivables look outstanding because they are between $300,000 and $350,000 – which means that the lender may lend from $240,000 to $275,000 to you based on this receivables asset.

Next, if the business is carrying three months of inventory – another asset – it may have $500,000 worth of good inventory and lender may lend $250,000 on that basis. You see that just two of business's assets may qualify you for as much as $500,000 in loans.

On top of this windfall, there are two other assets: machinery/equipment; real estate. The lender may lend 50% of the auction value of machinery and equipment and also lend 60-70% of a forced sell value on real estate.

As an additional example of how 'buying with little money' of your own works, I purchased Aetna Pipe Products of Illinois in 1983, which had annual revenue of $2,000,000 approximately per year. My purchase price was around $850,000. Why lay out that whole amount from my own pocket (assuming I had it)? I invested $85,000 of my own money, the bank lent me $765,000 to purchase, and made additional capital available to me of about $50,000. This way, I bought my first business with very little of my own money.

This example is a buyout and keep in mind that all transactions are different. Formulas are different. Lenders are different. If there are venture capitalists involved, they may lend more on the cash flow of business and not at all on assets like traditional banks would do. All lenders have their formulas and internal rules for lending.

*Buying a Business with No Money*

Yes, buying with no money of your own is also possible.

When we say buying with no money means simply that: You do not invest any of your own money. In this type of funding:

- the seller may keep money in the company's account which he is selling
- the seller may get an earnout
- the seller may get the note you will pay ongoing
- the seller may retain part of the business and keep the upside.
- the seller may take a royalty on business based on gross revenue

94

- the seller may get a consulting contract from you or agree not to compete for a period where business keeps paying seller.

Here are some specific areas where the seller sells to you, and you do not pay any of your own money at closing:

If the seller owns the real estate of business, he may sell the business and take the selling price as a note. The buyer keeps paying the purchase price (monthly, quarterly or as agreed for the debt). The seller has thus sold the business and not the real estate; the seller then rents that real estate to the buyer. This way, the seller gets rental income from the property, from the new owner's monthly payment on rent. This happens if the seller is convinced that the buyer could operate the business, and he continues getting rent and mortgage on the note.

If the seller is a large conglomerate and selling a small losing division, it may be advisable for the seller to sell on a note or earn-out to avoid any shutdown liabilities of the business. Many times, when a company shuts down, it triggers a 'shut down liabilities' action for the transaction. These liabilities can be diverse: Accrued payroll, employee vacations, unfunded pension liabilities, etc. Shutting down larger businesses may require giving notice to some regulatory agencies before closing. If it is a large company, shutting down a business might give them a bad reputation. If the seller does not get any money from a sale, but the buyer continues to operate this business and assumes all liabilities, then the seller avoids most or all shutdown liabilities. When a losing business is sold, it stops all the losses immediately; it stops bleeding cash.

If there is an environmental problem with the business, and the seller cannot handle it or it is too expensive for him, the buyer may buy the company fairly easily. The buyer operates it and works with EPA authorities.

If a business is continually losing money, and it has a loan, the lender loses confidence in the operator, owner. The lender may call in the loan and start the foreclosure process. The lender can continue losing money in these cases, as the owner of the business does not cooperate. Under these circumstances, a buyer could assume the loan and gives the lender a higher comfort level; in other words, a buyer steps into the owner's shoes. The buyer assumes the loan but does not pay any cash to either seller or lender.

If borrowable assets are far more than just a purchase price and a lender has faith in a buyer's reputation, the lender may then finance 100%. This happens only when they are confident that they will not lose money. The buyer does not need to pay any cash. The lender can always liquidate the business and get paid. 100% financing is typical in larger companies where there are lots of assets, but the business is losing money month after month. A new buyer comes up with a turnaround plan and makes the business profitable. This profitable business is created by first reducing expenses such as headcount, rent, and by dropping unprofitable parts of the company and second by improving and expanding the revenues. It is not uncommon to bring in a new profitable business or a new in-demand product line.

As examples of mine, when I bought Evron Industries out of bankruptcy, the business had enough assets where the lender lent me all the money. It had a large amount of inventory, enough good receivables, machinery and equipment, and building plant. Borrowing against all those assets covered more than the purchase price. If the business is under Chapter 11 bankruptcy, most of the accounts payable are not assumed. I bought this business with no money of my own. All funding came from different lenders.

When I purchased Gordon Brothers and also Sarah Michaels, financing on each business was on the inventory only. Dial Corporation was losing lots of money every month and offered us the business at an attractive price; this seller took a seller-financed note for the balance.

### *Buying with the Seller's Money*

Buying with a seller's money is a very common buyout. It may seem counterintuitive, but it happens all the time.

Depending on the seller, the seller may partially finance the business or finance it in full. I have bought several businesses that were seller financed and sold several businesses of my own, which I financed as seller.

You must approach it properly, and the seller should get comfortable that you will pay their full loan. Large companies also do it to get rid of their small divisions or product lines.

The amount of seller financing varies with the comfort level of each seller and your credentials. It also depends on what investment and expertise you bring to the business. Usually, seller-financed business purchases are simpler and easier ones than bank financed transactions. Seller financing is widespread for sellers who are retiring. If the seller does not have a successor, family member, or others, the seller may finance and get a monthly income from it. Sometimes, the seller wants to continue working and turns over control to the buyer with an employment contract.

If the business does not have hard liquid assets, the bank will not lend to the company; in these cases, the owner, if he wants to sell, usually finances.

A seller usually finances an unprofitable business or money-losing company, including sensitive environmental businesses and businesses in litigation.

As an example, I bought several businesses that were seller financed. Buffalo Tank, Bethlehem Supply, Vulcan Rivets and Bolt, Fitzgerald Railcar, Sarah Michaels, and a few others were all either partially or fully seller-financed. Many of them had a bank loan as a primary secured lender, but the seller typically financed a significant amount of the purchase price as a note. Evron's owner favored us because that owner/seller got a five-year contract with the business after I purchased it, with his salary paid to him as well.

Buying a Business with the Bank's Money

Every bank's business is to lend money and earn interest on it. That is all. If interest is high enough, the bank goes out of its way to lend you money. If you can convince the bank that their money is safe and you can pay the debt back, believe me, the bank wants to finance you. Usually, they want your money so that you, the borrower, have skin in the game, have some risk in the deal.

They have money – lots of money. Your money is not going to make any difference in their cash pile. Primarily, it will tie up your risk, so you make sure that business operates, and operates profitably, and you pay back their loan. If you have a proven track record, it becomes easier to convince banks to lend you most of the money. If a bank has a similar business under its portfolio that is performing well, it is easier for them to lend to you. Or if there is a business that is in default and the bank is going to foreclose, the bank will be willing to transfer the loan to you and hope that you will make them whole.

As an example, Evron Industries is a Chicago based company that was struggling due to substantial unsellable inventory and was losing money. One of their banks knew they would not be paid because the company's performance was deficient. In a short time, after we looked at the business, the business filed for bankruptcy. We purchased out of bankruptcy, and the previous bank stayed on for part of the loan.

If the business has a lot more assets that can be liquidated and the bank feels they do not have any risk, the bank may finance you all the way, 100% plus working capital, when you take over.

As another example, when I bought Bethlehem Supply it had lots of assets. It had large accounts receivable, a large inventory, several real estate locations owned all over the country. The bank noticed that it could quickly liquidate its assets and could recover their loan, so they financed all the credits and working capital.

If there is a seller's note which is subordinated to the bank, the bank becomes very comfortable. It goes out of its way to finance a business because if the company does not perform, the bank gets first right on all assets and comes out whole, or nearly whole.

An example is Buffalo Tank. When I bought it, Bethlehem Steel took a reasonably large-sized second position note. The fact that the seller took a note made the bank very comfortable, and so the bank financed most of the cash purchase price.

Buying at Market Price

You may think that buying at market price is no-brainer. If you pay market price or higher than the market price, in theory it becomes easier to buy a business. Well, yes and no: It is as tough as buying any other way described in this book. The purchase must still go through all the steps described in earlier chapters. You follow the steps, and you should be able to buy most of the companies which are for sale at market price or above.

Most of the time, these buyouts happen when a synergic buyer wants to purchase similar products and expand their business, or sometimes, you want to take a competitor out. Because by buying the target business, your volume and profit can be boosted significantly and in short order.

# Businesses the Author Acquired

1. Aetna Pipe Products of Illinois

2. Vulcan Rivets and Bolt Corporation

# 3.   Buffalo Tank Corporation

# 4.   Superior Welding Corporation

# 5.  Bethlehem Supply Corporation

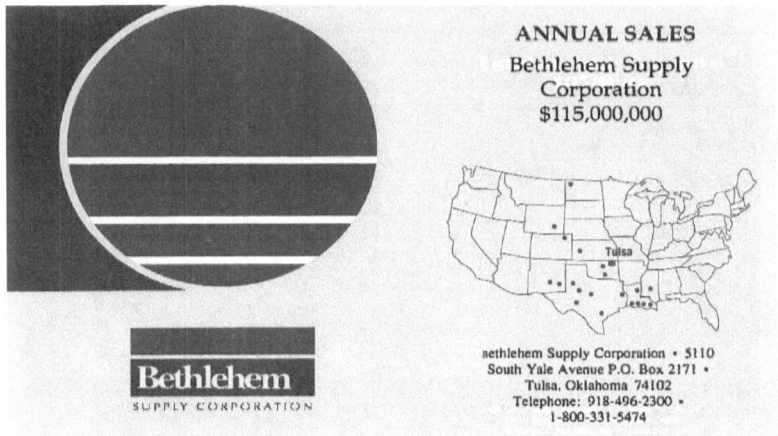

ANNUAL SALES

Bethlehem Supply
Corporation
$115,000,000

Bethlehem Supply Corporation • 5110
South Yale Avenue P.O. Box 2171 •
Tulsa, Oklahoma 74102
Telephone: 918-496-2300 •
1-800-331-5474

# 6.  Circleville Metal Works

# 7. Houston Steel Products

8. Freeman Company

9. San Francisco Soap Company

10. Fitzgerald Railcar Company

11. Gem Manufacturing Company

# 12. Kirks Castile Soap Company

# 13 Evron Industries LTD

# 14. Aelco Foundries

# 15. Computron Display Systems, Inc.

The Pilots of the World's Most Sophisticated Aircraft Rely on the Precision and Clarity of Computron Monitors.

Now You Can Too.

# 16. American Family Soap

# The Cevin Industry Philosophy...

*At Cevin our philosophy is simple, purposeful,*
*real - It's "Opportunity".*
*We aggressively seek opportunity!*
*Opportunity for all our associates.*
*The opportunity to succeed where others have failed.*
*The opportunity to compete, to strive for excellence - in our*
*products, services and relationships,*
*the opportunity to Change, Evolve and*
*Grow-both Individually and Corporately.*
*The opportunity to provide Jobs, Satisfaction, Fulfillment and Fun.*
*The Opportunity to profit and serve!*

*Our goals are High,*
*The Stakes are High,*
*The Rewards are High!*

K. J. Hathi
*Chairman of the board*

# About the Author

The author of this book, Ken Hathi, is from India. Hathi came to Columbus, Ohio, USA in 1968 as a graduate student in Electrical Engineering. He ran out of money while in school, dropped out of college and joined an instrumentation company as an electrical engineer in Long Island New York. He went back to India in 1970, got married and returned to the USA. Upon coming back, he lost his job due to cutbacks in the aerospace program. He worked with various small companies as an engineer and then joined Advanced Packaging which got purchased by a Chicago Tie wrap packaging company; he moved then with his wife to Chicago.

In Chicago, he joined a mighty conglomerate multinational company called Union Carbide. Hathi says "Working at Union Carbide trained me. I learnt manufacturing business, its efficiency, the ins and out of plants and production. It gave me confidence for rest of my life."

While at Union Carbide, he worked on varieties of its product lines such as Glad Bag, Preston Anti-Freeze, Viskase casing, disposable diapers and so on. Carbide thrived to be leader, no. 1 in every product it made. When

Carbide could not be leader, for instance, in the disposable diaper business against Pampers (a P & G product), Carbide asked Hathi to shut down that plant in Hartford Connecticut and asked him to relocate the plant and production to Union Carbide in Germany.

Hathi's family in India was a business family in Raval India, a tiny village on India's west coast. He was youngest of 13 children. Out of seven older brothers, four had migrated from Raval to Uganda East Africa before he was born. All brothers had established their own businesses individually in Uganda along with one sister and her husband. Two other brothers and four sisters were all in business in India. Only one brother worked as a salaried civil engineer in India and later migrated to London and the USA.

So, Hathi grew up with business and with business talk. Hathi says he enjoyed working at Union Carbide, it was great company to work for. He travelled all over USA built and started their plants and product lines. He learnt business and brand name from carbide. All was fine, he had dream job and good salary benefits and everything what one dreams for.

However, he was not satisfied – he wanted to own his own business; business was in his genes. The comfort of paycheck and security was so good, so he kept working there for 10 years.

While working at Carbide, he lived on Chicago's north side. They had a daughter born around that time. He lived upstairs of a private house, downstairs the owner lived. Owner was a factory worker, after so many years of hard work he had bought a two-story house which was his pride and joy. Every day and weekend the landlord worked around the house, he was proud of his castle and Hathi respected it. Soon after they moved in, the landlord started complaining about everything. Hathi's daughter is crying, Mr. and Mrs. Hathi are coming in and out late, Mr. and Mrs. Hathi are noisy, Mr. and Mrs. Hathi make his carpeted stairs messy and so on...It became un tolerable. So, Hathi started looking for another apartment and while looking to rent in Logan Square, he came across an apartment to rent. The landlord says yes, she will rent it to him, but she was also selling the building. Hathi inquired about the price and after a few discussions, he (along with a friend) bought his first 12 flat building with $5,000 down and a $70,000 purchase price. The seller was moving to Florida and needed monthly income, so she financed me. After moving in to one of the apartments, Hathi realized, after paying all the expenses and mortgage, and living rent-free he had some leftover income.

This set off his apartment building buying spree! In few years, he'd purchased five to six buildings with total of 120 or so units, all on the north side of Chicago. All the buildings were financed by the sellers. Once he had one building, it became easier to buy other buildings as he did not need to go to banks.

Hathi did not yet realize that this was a business, and that he could grow big in Real Estate. Business to him was like Union Carbide and other commercial, product-producing businesses. Product, plant, and equipment.

Hathi did not know anything of buying a business; he knew, though, about operations, plants, and the manufacturing of products.

During that time, Hathi also owned a small hotel in Michigan City Indiana, about 60 miles away from his home in Chicago. One day he met a guest there. He knew that Hathi was good at factories and production equipment. He then introduced me with a friend of his who was buying a manufacturing business in Chicago. The buyer, his friend, wanted Hathi's help to analyze the condition of machinery and equipment. It was small company cutting and threading pipes for lamp industry; the machinery was adequate for the business. To make the story short, right in middle of negotiations, the seller died, the buyer backed out. The bank where the business's accounts were, called Hathi and asked if he would like to buy that business saying the bank will finance him. He was so eager to go in his own business, that he agreed and bought his first manufacturing Company, Aetna Pipe Company of Illinois.

The company was well established for 50 plus years, with a business to business product line in the lamp and lighting industry, 20 plus employees, two plants and nationwide sales and distribution.

By tweaking here and there, the company became very profitable. The business had experienced employees and manager for 30 plus years, so it did not need Hathi to do much! It was great buy; Hathi was making more monthly profit than his yearly salary at Union Carbide. He loved it and left Union Carbide in 1984.

As time went by, all income at Aetna Pipe was piling up and burning hole in his pockets. His loan at the bank to buyout the company got paid up in a year or soon after that. This established a great reputation with the bank also of his ability to service debt and operate manufacturing company.

Very soon, Hathi thought of expanding Aetna Pipe business. He came across a building for sale in Birmingham Alabama. When he went to look at it, it was an operating fasteners business of Bethlehem Steel named Vulcan Rivet and Bolt. It was five times larger in annual revenue than Aetna Pipe with 100,000 plus square feet plant and 100 plus employees. Hathi was duly impressed and fascinated with the business. He bought that business in 1985. First Chicago Bank financed the business with just a small down payment.

The business was a sinking ship, losing money every month. Hathi worked hard, automated machines, streamlined material flow, reduced unprofitable product lines, and reduced head counts. In couple of years, company turned the corner and became profitable. Bethlehem Steel was incredibly happy with him, that he could operate and turn around their losing business. They had number of loser businesses which they wanted to offload but there were no takers. So they approached Hathi again and offered Buffalo Tank corporation with six plants and a $30 Million annual revenue. It was also big loser but MNC Commercial at Baltimore MD financed Hathi for it. After that, Hathi did not stop, but bought Bethlehem Supply Company with 27 locations and $200 Million annual revenue. He was on a business buying spree! From 1983 starting from scratch, to 1990, Hathi acquired ten plus businesses, with 30 plus locations, and whopping annual revenue of $200 Million plus!

Well after that, a big industry and economic downturn came in the late 1980s and Hathi's businesses suffered setbacks like so many others. Banks were going out of business; Resolution Trust of Federal government was taking over banks left and right. Most of his loans was with various banks, and due to their situation, they called the loan. To pay off loans, Hathi sold and liquidated number of businesses which had heavy debt during that tough time.

Hathi had few businesses left so restarted again in 90s. Previously his businesses were too concentrated in the capital goods market, so he started diversifying in consumer products, medical equipment, data processing and transportation.

He bought a bar soap company from P&G, a skin care and hair care company from Dial Corporation, a medical equipment company, a railcar company from Cargill, a data processing company and so on. In 25 years starting in 1983, Hathi acquired, owned and operated 25 or so businesses altogether. It was wild ride of business buying spree and selling sprees as well. Hathi had decided to retire at the age of 65 and sold the last operating business Fitzgerald Railcar in 2008.

Those 25 years of continually active business buying were enjoyable to him though he had setbacks and some losses, but it was a numbers game. It did not slow Hathi down. He was never a top-down owner or manager who looks at sales accounting and management. He was rather a bottom-up owner and manager who walked through every plant, enjoyed the products and product lines, talked and worked with employees on the plant floor and who knew many of them by first name.

Now as Hathi retired, his friends and their children, as well as his own children ask his advice all the time: "How did you do it?" and, to answer them, he wrote this book.

He is looking forward writing a number of other books such as, "How to operate a business" "My business memoirs and stories", "How to negotiate a buyout" "Business pleasures, problems and sleepless nights" and so on.

For further information, please visit K J Hathi's website:

www.howtobuybusiness.com

His Email: support@howtobuybusiness.com

Here's the direct link for his Kindle book:

https://www.amazon.com/dp/B086R4GZGT

For his paperback, go to:

https://www.amazon.com/dp/B08762T2TB

# Press Releases about Author's Purchases

In 2020, here is what still popped up on a Google search of "K.J. Hathi" about one of his first purchases: It made headlines at the time!

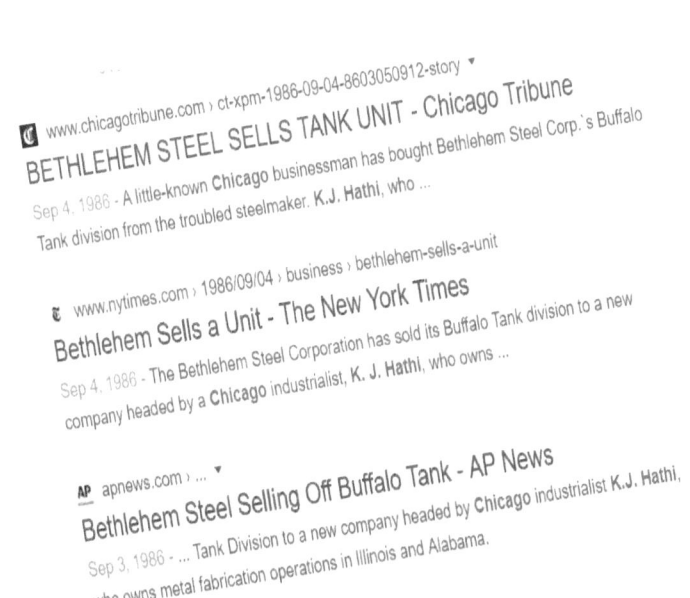

# PIPE DREAM

*When the big boys of industry unload their losers,*
*Ken Hathi is there, snapping up winners*

*by* LISA KARTUS

Last year, when Bethlehem Steel announced its first profit since 1981, its chairman, Walter Williams, was crowing to Ken Hathi, chief of Oak Brook–based Cevin Industries. Hathi was impressed, but took the opportunity to tease Williams: "I told Walt that part of the glory goes to me, because I bought their losers," Hathi says, laughing.

In jest there is truth. Since about 1982, companies like Bethlehem have been restructuring, divesting themselves of profit-draining operations. And in the past five years Hathi, a man with an infectious laugh and a down-to-earth notion of automation, has bought five small heavy-industrial companies with total sales of $180 million, three of them from Bethlehem Steel. It's too soon to tell on the latest two, but it looks as if he's been able to help turn around three unprofitable businesses.

Four, if you count Bethlehem.

In a way, Hathi's is an old-fashioned American immigrant success story. He came to this country 20 years ago from Porbandar, India (where Gandhi was born), to pursue a master's degree in electrical engineering at Ohio State University. He eventually landed at Union Carbide, where he worked for ten years, automating their Glad Bag plant, among others. It taught him more than school ever did.

"When you talk automation, people think of robots doing the work," says Hathi. "That's not real life. Real life is automatic material flow, that is as good or better than robots, because it gets done by itself. You don't have someone looking like a human being and doing things like a human being as long as you can achieve the end result without touching the product." When you're not spending money on either robots or humans, you save money. And, paradoxically, when you automate a failing plant you save jobs, because it doesn't shut down completely.

In 1983, his last year at Carbide, Hathi had his bankers help him look for a company to buy. They came up with Aetna Pipe.

"Talk about Rust Belt," he says. "You can't get any lower tech than cutting and threading pipe." Main Bank advanced $520,000 of the $600,000 purchase price against Aetna's equipment, receivables, inventory, and real estate. Hathi put in $80,000 he had invested in apartment buildings, and took over a 60-year-old company in a tired West Side neighborhood, with 30 employees making mundane products on antiquated machines.

Hathi computerized the office. He put out a catalogue. He got an 800 telephone number. And he hooked some of those antiquated machines together using sensors and levers. Aetna now makes a profit on its $2.5-million annual sales.

It was a comfortable business to run. After all, "I could fix almost all of the machines," Hathi says. But he quickly got bored. Leafing through an acquisitions newsletter, he noticed a company for sale in Birmingham, Alabama. "When I contacted the right party, I found that it was a part of Bethlehem Steel, making fasteners," he says. Don't picture snaps and zippers. Vulcan Rivet & Bolt Corporation made the sort of fasteners that join the beams of high-rise buildings. Sales were about eight million dollars a

Ken Hathi, chief of Oak Brook–based Cevin Industries: "When you talk automation," he says, "people think of robots. That's not real life."

*Illustration:* CATHIE BLECK *photograph:* PETER ROSENBAUM

120

## EXECS

year, but Bethlehem was losing money on the operation.

Hathi took over, cut the number of employees from 85 to 50, cut back on some of the product line, and automated. "The Birmingham plant was perfect for automation. You put raw material in on one side and it comes out finished product on the other side," he says.

The trick was keeping it simple. "Say you have a machine built in 1930. [Hathi's youngest plant is 60 years old.] At that time there were no transistors, no electronics. There were some controls to turn the machine on and off, but then once that piece of product is made, there was no means of sensing that it was finished. And there was no means to automatically go to the next step. I'm connecting the machines with sensors and putting automatic conveying on other machines," he says.

After Hathi turned Vulcan into a money-maker, he offered to buy Bethlehem's money-losing Lebanon, Pennsylvania, fastener plant, one of the largest plants of its kind in the country. "They threw me out, saying I was too small," Hathi recalls. "Well, guess what happened after a year? They closed it down, auctioned it off, and all the employees lost their jobs. Bethlehem took a $30-million hit." You see, when companies close plants, they still have to pay severance and contributions toward employee pensions and medical liability. When they sell a plant to an outsider like Hathi, he takes on those problems.

Maybe that's why, in 1986, it was Bethlehem that approached Hathi about buying one of their most persistent losers. Buffalo Tank, with six plants, was the industry leader in underground storage tanks, and also made things like 126-foot-long autoclaves. It consistently lost three to four million dollars annually on sales of $30 million. After three years of trying to sell Buffalo, Bethlehem was about to close it down, when Hathi agreed to acquire it for ten million dollars. "They took some financing, expecting that they would never see the money paid back," Hathi says, "but at least they wouldn't have the shutdown cost. Well, in a year they had a surprise. They got paid up."

It was Hathi's biggest reach. And it took 18 months to turn it around.

"We had to change the top management," Hathi says. "With experience I had come to the conclusion that if a company is losing money, no matter what the reason, the top guys are directly and exclusively responsible for it. It's their job to make sure

that the productivity is there, that the material is purchased at the right price, that the marketing and selling is done right." Hathi's new management quickly came up with four new products—four times as many as Buffalo Tank had developed in the previous 20 years. He raised prices, cut the number of employees from 280 to 175, discontinued custom work, and created an assembly-line operation at the Baltimore plant.

Also in 1986, Hathi paid three million dollars to buy Superior Welding, of Decatur, Illinois, from the Varien Corporation. Superior makes big pressure vessels for refineries and chemical and food plants, and has annual sales of about six million dollars. Then this past December Bethlehem Steel was back, and Hathi acquired Bethlehem Supply, operator of 19 retail outlets that function as hardware stores to oil-patch companies such as Exxon, a customer for many years. Last year Bethlehem Supply had sales of about $80 million; this year Hathi expects to reach $110 million.

Since Hathi's purchases are 80 to 100 percent leveraged, does he ever lose sleep, worrying about owing millions of dollars?

"Nope. I sleep very well. My brother-in-law is a physician, and he can't believe that when I decide not to think about anything, I don't think about anything. Zero. It blanks out," Hathi says.

"What people get carried away with is the idea that, now that they've got $100 million, their lives are more valuable," he says. "But if you get down to the basics, you're still going to ride in the same car on the same crazy highways, fly in the same plane, have the same risk of cancer—you know, anything can happen," he says, shrugging.

Is this Indian fatalism here? "Yes, maybe it is. There is a Sanskrit teaching that your job is to do things the way you think is best, without expecting results or thinking about results. If it doesn't come out, fine," says Hathi. "The end result is not in my control. Then you'll not feel sorry about things. And in that respect, if a company fails—because, statistically, some of the companies are going to fail, it's just a matter of time—then I accept that; then I would not regret it that much. But my job is to keep trying to make sure that it does not fail," Hathi says: After all, "my reputation is on the line."  ~

*Lisa Kartus is co-owner of Financial News Bureau/Midwest, in Chicago.*

121

# He buys 'em out, fixes 'em up, makes 'em work

By Frederick H. Lowe

Ken Hathi, chief executive officer of Oak Brook-based Cevin Industries, admits that some union leaders don't like what he does when he buys a business.

"Some of the companies are losing money and I have to lay people off in order to cut costs," he said.

But his solution is better than the alternative, he insisted. "If those businesses had remained with their parent companies, there wouldn't be any jobs to argue about because the plants probably would have been closed."

Hathi, a former electrical engineer with Union Carbide, buys companies that are considered part of mature industries, or businesses that are in markets expected to show only a minimal amount of growth. Such businesses are usually at the top of the plant closing lists.

He takes such castoffs and streamlines and modernizes them so they either turn a profit or make more money. So far, he's come up with a winning plan.

Cevin, a holding company for three firms—Buffalo Tank of Baltimore, Bethlehem Steel Supply Corp. of Tulsa, Okla., and Superior Welding Co. of Decatur, Ill.—is expected to gross more than $175 million in 1988.

Since 1986, Hathi, who owns 80 percent of Cevin, has purchased three Bethlehem Steel divisions. The most recent acquisition took place two weeks ago, when Hathi bought Bethlehem Steel Supply

> **If those businesses had remained with their parent companies, there wouldn't be any jobs to argue about because the plants probably would have been closed.**

Corp., a company that sells oil field drilling equipment throughout the Southwest.

"In 1986, the company had revenues of $65 million. Last year, it had sales of $87 million and a couple of years ago it had sales of $300 million. So you see the company's sales have been all over the map," he explained.

It was sold because Bethlehem Steel would have had to invest $30 million into the division to make its

earnings more consistent. "Bethlehem Steel doesn't want to do that, because the company is only a small part of a $4 billion business," Hathi said.

Bethlehem Steel spokesman Henry Von H. Spruckelsen agreed: "If we invested in Bethlehem Steel Supply, it would take money away from our core business of steel manufacturing."

Since 1985, Hathi also has purchased Buffalo Tank Corp. of Baltimore, and Vulcan Rivet & Bolt from Bethlehem Steel. Vulcan he purchased himself, not for Cevin Industries.

Modernization is his key to bringing Vulcan and the Cevin companies to ultimate profitability. Hathi buys modern equipment, and once the factory begins to earn money, profits are reinvested back into the plant. He sticks with companies involved in basic industry, because he's leery of high-tech companies.

"I use to automate plants for Union Carbide and I'm aware of what will and will not work," he explained.

When Hathi buys a company, he also makes sure he owns the name. "The name has a lot of value. It has credibility and it's a big asset for the business," he said.

Despite grumbling from some union officials, Hathi said his relations with them are good. "When we have layoffs, they are usually just temporary. Once we start making money, we call them back," he said.

Ken Hathi, chief executive of Cevin Industries, general businesses near the top of somebody's shutdown list.

# Intended buyer: Trucks still key

**By PAUL DODSON**
Tribune Business Writer

The president of the company proposing to buy AM General Corp.'s South Bend plant said he intends to aggressively seek out new truck business to keep the plant busy.

While U.S. military truck business will be sought, the proposed new owner will place a strong emphasis on exporting trucks to foreign military forces.

K.J. Hathi, president of Cevin Industries Inc., Oak Brook, Ill., was interviewed by telephone Thursday following his company's announcement earlier in the day that it intended to purchase the huge South Bend factory building and the AM General medium and heavy truck business from LTV Corp. of Dallas.

AM General had announced a year ago that it was quitting the medium and heavy military truck business and would concentrate on building the Hummer vehicle for the U.S. Defense Department. The Hummer, a light truck, is produced at AM General's Mishawaka plant.

In announcing its departure from the heavy and medium truck business, AM General had said it would close its South Bend plant. Cevin Industries' announcement Thursday indicated the company intends to keep the plant in operation.

However, Hathi said Thursday that he does not yet know how many people would be employed at the South Bend plant.

Cevin Industries would not take

See AM GENERAL /Page A11

# AM GENERAL
from Page A1

over the current work force at the South Bend plant, according to an AM General spokesman, but it is likely that the new owner would seek to hire people who had worked there or who had vehicle-building experience with the former owners.

The South Bend AM General plant now employs 575 hourly workers. Most of these workers have more seniority than workers at the Hummer plant. This means that most of the South Bend workers can "bump" employees with less seniority.

Hathi emphasized his company intends to retain the AM General name.

His company issued a prepared statement which said, "AM General has been a world-renowned manufacturer of military vehicles. It is the purchaser's intent to take over all of AM General's existing medium and heavy truck business and continue this proud heritage of AM General."

Hathi added, "AM General in the past had exported a large quantity of trucks and we want to get back into that marketplace. A weaker dollar will help, also.

"In certain Mideast and Far East countries, AM General has sold lots of trucks. These are two marketplaces where we again hope to very heavily sell some more trucks," he said.

"AM General's name lends such credibility. They are a world leader. In some countries, they want nothing but AM General trucks. We will capitalize on the good name enjoyed in the past," he said.

Building trucks represents a new field for Cevin Industries, said Hathi, who is principal stockholder. Three companies owned by Cevin Industries employ more than 600 people. All of the companies are engaged in manufacturing.

These companies include Buffalo Tank Corp., which is based in Jacksonville, Fla., and which has operations in Baltimore, Wooster, Mass., Romulus, Mich., and Charlotte and Raleigh, N.C.

Buffalo Tank makes underground storage tanks, used primarily by service stations, and does other custom metal-fabricating work.

Other companies owned by Cevin Industries include Superior Welding Corp., Decatur, Ill.; and Aetna Pipe Products Co., Chicago.

Hathi said he also owns Vulcan Rivet & Bolt Corp., Birmingham, Ala. However, Vulcan is not a part of Cevin Industries.

Hathi said Cevin Industries has been in business for five years but companies it owns each have been in business for more than 50 years.

Craig Mac Nab, a spokesman for AM General, had said Thursday that Cevin Industries has made its reputation on buying troubled manufacturing plants and nurturing them back to health.

Hathi is an American citizen who came to the U.S. about 20 years ago from Porbandar, India. He came here to obtain a master's degree in electrical engineering from Ohio State University and later was employed for 10 years by Union Carbide Co.

He went into business for himself in 1983 by purchasing Aetna Pipe from Bethlehem Steel Co.

123

# A toast is raised for AM General

**PAUL DODSON**
ON THE BUSINESS BEAT

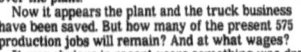

It was wonderful to learn the AM General truck factory has a good chance of remaining alive.

For nearly a year, since AM General Corp. announced it would quit the medium- and heavy-duty truck business, the threat of death has been hanging over the plant.

Now it appears the plant and the truck business have been saved. But how many of the present 575 production jobs will remain? And at what wages?

It was obvious in recent years something was drastically wrong at AM General. First it was the loss of the Postal Service vehicle business that had been a mainstay for many years. And then it was the loss of the 5-ton Army truck business, the other mainstay.

Perhaps Cevin Industries Inc., the company proposing to buy the AM General truck business and the South Bend plant, can find a way to revitalize the operation.

K.J. Hathi, president of Cevin Industries, who is originally from India, sounds like a man with global vision. In his first interview with this newspaper, Hathi announced he plans to aggressively seek out new work for the plant, with a special emphasis on international sales.

The Oak Brook, Ill.-based Cevin Industries is a young business, just six years old, with a history of buying aged and failing manufacturing operations and turning them around.

According to the October issue of Chicago magazine, Hathi has purchased five small manufacturing companies since 1983.

In purchasing the South Bend truck plant, it is clear Cevin Industries is not taking the present AM General workers along with the deal. But it is likely that Cevin Industries will be eager to hire former AM General workers. After all, they have experience in building military vehicles.

It is good for the community that the truck plant will remain in operation. The last thing this town needs is another big, empty factory building. Many people will benefit, aside from the direct employment, because the truck plant buys many millions of dollars of year in goods and services locally.

There were some interesting quotes in the Chicago magazine article which provides insight into the way Hathi thinks.

It quoted him as saying, "When you talk automation, people think of robots doing the work. Real life is automatic material flow, that is as good or better than robots, because it gets done by itself ... When you're not spending money on either robots or humans, you save money. And, paradoxically, when you automate a failing plant, you save jobs, because it doesn't shut down completely."

The article also quoted Hathi as saying: "With experience I had come to the conclusion that if a company is losing money, no matter what the reason, the top guys are directly and exclusively responsible for it. It's their job to make sure that the productivity is there, that the material is purchased at the right price, that the marketing and selling is done right."

He sounds tough and smart. And he sounds like a winner.

Welcome to South Bend, Mr. Hathi. Here's hoping it will be a good marriage.